LEARNING TO LEAD

FOURTH EDITION

LEARNING TO LEAD

A Workbook on Becoming a Leader

WARREN BENNIS

JOAN GOLDSMITH

BASIC
BOOKS

A Member of the Perseus Books Group

NEW YORK

Copyright © 2010 by Warren Bennis and Joan Goldsmith
Published by Basic Books,
A Member of the Perseus Books Group

Books published by Basic Books are available at special discounts for bulk purchases
in the United States by corporations, institutions, and other organizations. For more
information, please contact the Special Markets Department at the Perseus Books
Group, 2300 Chestnut Street, Suite 200, Philadelphia, PA 19103, or call (800) 810-4145,
ext. 5000, or e-mail special.markets@perseusbooks.com.

Library of Congress Cataloging-in-Publication Data

Bennis, Warren G.
  Learning to lead : a workbook on becoming a leader / Warren Bennis, Joan Goldsmith.
      p. cm.
  Includes bibliographical references and index.
  ISBN 978-0-465-01886-4 (alk. paper)
  1. Leadership. 2. Management. I. Goldsmith, Joan. II. Title.
  HD57.7.B463 2010
  658.4'092--dc22
                        2010003801

10 9 8 7 6 5 4 3 2

For our grandchildren, the leaders of our future,
may you realize your dreams:

For Luke and Anya; Devin and Daniel;
Nathaniel and Oliver; Eliana and Abraham,
WITH LOVE FROM *Warren and Grace*

For Orrin and Thacher and Tallulah; Soraya and Alana,
WITH LOVE FROM *Joan and Ken*

CONTENTS

PREFACE

Of course, the answer to the slavery question was already embedded within our Constitution—a Constitution that had at its very core the ideal of equal citizenship under the law; a Constitution that promised its people liberty, and justice, and a union that could be and should be perfected over time.

And yet words on a parchment would not be enough to deliver slaves from bondage, or provide men and women of every color and creed their full rights and obligations as citizens of the United States. What would be needed were Americans in successive generations who were willing to do their part—through protests and struggle, on the streets and in the courts, through a civil war and civil disobedience and always at great risk—to narrow that gap between the promise of our ideals and the reality of their time. . . . I believe deeply that we cannot solve the challenges of our time unless we solve them together—unless we perfect our union by understanding that we may have different stories, but we hold common hopes; that we may not look the same and we may not have come from the same place, but we all want to move in the same direction—towards a better future for our children and our grandchildren.

> **—Senator Barack Obama**
>
> **"A More Perfect Union," speech on patriotism, delivered March 18, 2008**

It has been eighteen years since we first published *Learning to Lead* and although we have witnessed many changes during that time, we have never wavered in our certainty that we continually require leadership to confront turbulent times as well as personal upheavals in our daily lives. The leaders of today who meet challenges both on the international stage and in their own communities have certain clear and identifiable qualities.

They are both reflective and action-oriented. They understand that collaboration produces the most creative and effective outcomes. They take pleasure in encouraging others to succeed and flourish. They make decisions even when all the data are not available. They are not afraid to refrain from action when restraint seems warranted. They generate and sustain trust, and are purveyors of hope, while not fanning unrealistic expectations. They encourage transparency and eschew the use of fear. They are wholly and actively people of principle. They find joy and fulfillment in solving problems. They consistently discourage "personality cults" and shy away from monuments to their achievements. They seek to learn, for the sheer pleasure of it. They are committed to shaping the learning of others, especially those who are in most need of a chance to learn. They prepare the ground of acceptance for what has not yet been imagined, a trait especially important in an age as fluid and uncertain as ours. They are imaginative as well as practical. They relish diversity and they are instinctively compassionate toward those with whom they differ.

You, our reader, may feel we are asking too much of you when we suggest that you strive to match these leadership attributes. But if you elect to do so, we promise you that you will ennoble your life and increase your joy in living it. We are each longtime students of leadership and have found the learning process both challenging and satisfying.

Warren was dramatically confronted with the demand to be a leader as one of the youngest lieutenants in the U.S. army in the European Theater during World War II. He not only led his men into combat but sought to guide foot soldiers toward an understanding and appreciation of the values they were defending with their lives. His leadership lessons emerged during his stint as university president and, more recently, in his capacity as Distinguished Professor at the University of Southern California and Chair of the Board of Advisors for the Center for Public Leadership at Harvard University's Kennedy School of Government. His role as advisor to many public- and private-sector leaders seeking and engaging the highest offices in corporations, city governments, Congress, and presidential administrations provided opportunities for Warren to share the lessons he learned and the wisdom he gathered.

Joan was shaped as a leader by the civil rights struggles in Chicago in the 1960s and, later, during the desegregation of Boston's public schools. As a faculty member at Harvard University's Graduate School of Education she confronted leadership challenges in attempts to reduce racial and gender discrimination among students and staff. Her leadership lessons were hard-won; as a founder of Cambridge College, she learned strategies for encouraging women and professionals of color as successful leaders in positions they had previously been denied.

As we both to reflect on leadership in this fourth edition of *Learning to Lead*, we invite you to join us in gaining new insights in a critical effort to make a difference in troubled times.

A Time of Crisis

In the beginning of this new century, the deck has been shuffled and wildcards have been added over and over again. Changing rules have turned our world topsy-turvy, bringing dramatic new players to the stage.

Consider, for example, the change that occurred in Philadelphia, Mississippi, the small community where in 1964 the Ku Klux Klan killed three civil rights workers in one of the era's most infamous crimes. Forty-five years later, in 2009, the mostly white populace of this city elected a black mayor, James A. Young, to lead them. Recently the Xerox corporation announced that their first female CEO, Anne Mulcahy, an anomaly in corporate leadership herself, had retired and replaced herself with Ursula Burns, the first African-American woman to lead a corporation of this size.

On the international scene, China has embraced entrepreneurism and other forms of capitalism and has emerged as a player, fiercely contending with India to be the premier "emerging market." The European Union is now a global economic force, replacing the franc and deutsche mark with the Esperanto of European currencies, the euro. And Latin American leaders, having emerged from very poor communities and previously unempowered ethnic minorities, are increasingly independent in their political and economic leanings, often shunning the United States and its history of economic and political leadership.

Inside the United States, the rules of the game are in flux. At Google and other giants in Silicon Valley, over 50 percent of engineers are immigrants (primarily from India, China, and Russia) and they are transforming this segment of U.S. industry into the world's leading producer of wealth and new jobs. The American free press is in danger of extinction, as well-respected newspapers including the *Boston Globe* and the *Los Angeles Times* drastically cut editorial and other staff, consider Web-based outlets, and take extreme measures to avoid bankruptcy. In addition, diversity of opinion and reporting assignments have narrowed as media conglomerates buy and sell news organizations to finance capital investments.

The "new economy" that emerged and soared in the 1990s has now crashed. The auto industry and vendors, suppliers, and adjacent industries in the United States are bankrupt or close to it. Once-respected corporate leaders have been accused of unbridled greed and irresponsible manipulation of financial deregulation. The worldwide economic crisis, the worst since the Great Depression of the 1930s, has revealed failures in the interlocking system of markets, stock exchanges, investment networks, and banks. Headlines from the *New York Times* scream disaster in graphic terms:

- Bush White House Leaves $482 Billion Deficit
- Lehman Hit Hard as Talks End
- One Week's Wild Ride: A Vast Economic Bailout as U.S. Acts to Restore Confidence

- Super-Rich Getty Trust to Slash Its Budget 25%
- Asian Investors Fear Aftershocks of U.S. Meltdown
- A Bitter Struggle Over Outsize Pay for Executives
- Central Banks' Lifeline: Huge Loans Attempt to Spur Revival of Lending
- A Fragile, Lonely Existence for Remaining Wall St. Titans: Morgan Stanley Seeks Merger; Goldman Feels Pressure
- Shaken British Leader Gordon Brown Fights to Stay at Helm
- 60,000 Jobs Lost in a Single Day: The Cuts by Firms such as Caterpillar, GM and Home Depot Aren't Likely to Reverse Under a Stimulus Plan
- In the Lap of Luxury, Paris Squirms and Faces Most Serious Setback Since War Broke in 1939
- Forecasters See Fast Recovery; Others Doubt Their Eyesight
- Data Shows Manufacturing Is Suffering in All Corners
- Stocks Rally to Start Year; Will January Be an Omen?

President Obama has labeled abhorrent business practices "shameful and the height of irresponsibility." Joseph Stiglitz, the 2001 Nobel Laureate in economics, estimated that the rate of worldwide unemployment for 2009 could reach 50 million. Mary Schapiro, upon becoming president of the Securities and Exchange Commission (SEC), uncovered spiraling fraud in the billions perpetrated by the corporations her agency was responsible for monitoring. The exposure of the shocking "Ponzi" scheme of once-respected financier Bernard Madoff revealed that he had stolen $65 billion from a network of trusting individuals, universities, hedge funds, and charitable organizations in phantom investments perpetrated over thirteen years.

These hard-to-believe scandals have continued to unfold in failing world finances. Shortly after the banking and investment giant Citigroup received an initial bailout with U.S. taxpayer funds, its executives allocated $50 million to purchase a corporate jet. Richard Fuld Jr., the chief executive of Lehman Brothers, who hid and disguised the financial ruin of his company and oversaw the bankruptcy of this once-venerable institution, received $466 million from 1993 to 2008 in personal compensation and $62 million in exit pay. Charles Prince, chief executive of Citigroup, who oversaw his bank's near failure, earned $53 million from 2003 to 2007 and $40 million in exit pay. James Cayne, chief executive of Bear Stearns, who headed this investment bank as it crumbled and was taken over by the U.S. government in an attempt to save it, earned $232 million from 1993 to 2007 and $61 million in exit pay. Equally astonishing was the report from more than two dozen high-ranking Freddie Mac executives that CEO Richard Syron ignored their internal warnings on the danger of sub-prime mortgages and derivatives they gave him as early as 2004. Syron earned $19.8 million in 2007 as his company was sliding into ruin.

Outrageous amounts of compensation for heads of failing banks are disheartening enough in times of financial despair, but when we realize that these banks misspent the retirement accounts of working people, cost the thin mortgages of poor families, and misspent the scrimped savings of countless millions, we question not only those who greedily took the money but also the board members, consultants, advisors, and government regulators who were complicit in such shameful practices.

Economic failure has impacted once-protected civil service employees who face layoffs and furloughs without pay in state, county, and city governments, and has threatened the stability of big-city public school systems attempting to avoid bankruptcy. Unemployment is at its highest in decades, hiring freezes are mounting, and urban core populations face home foreclosures and an epidemic of youth who are living on the street.

The Los Angeles County food bank that supplies meals for the needy reported delivering 750,000 meals a week in the spring of 2009 for a population swelling with the elderly and a growing number of middle-class families. This figure has ballooned since that date as food supplies diminish. A national deficit threatens social and medical protection for children, the poor, and the elderly. Political conflicts surrounding the adoption of a new U.S. healthcare system have blocked widespread and thorough coverage for needy populations. The income gap between the wealthy and those without hope for minimum subsistence grows daily.

The American Dream is crumbling as those in communities across the country lose their homes, their jobs, and their pensions, and are relegated to living in the street, in the largest numbers since the Great Depression.

Heads of households wonder: Can we remain employed and stabilize our personal finances? Can we feed and clothe our families and ourselves? Can we maintain healthcare coverage and meet mortgage payments? The ruptured economy is particularly painful for rural Americans. They wonder: can we meet fuel prices we cannot afford and can we heat our homes, power our trucks and farm equipment, feed our livestock, transport our children to schools, and take our family members to doctors and drive for errands to grocery and hardware stores. Many are finding it increasingly difficult to meet the everyday requirements of a simple life.

Despite the highest medical expenditures in the world, the United States is currently ranked twenty-ninth in the world in infant mortality rate, tied with Poland and Slovakia and far behind many Scandinavian and East Asian countries. Yet large U.S. pharmaceuticals, insurance companies, and medical conglomerates have strenuously opposed healthcare reform for newborn children.

Technology, that magnificent tool, allows people worldwide to communicate electronically, bringing down walls that once separated nations and facilitating the exchange of ideas among individuals. However, it has not made life safer or more peaceful. Religious fundamentalists have turned the most up-to-date machines to medieval uses. We now live in a world where the suffering of a woman being stoned to death for adultery can be broadcast on satellite TV, where cell phones can be used to detonate bombs and data from confidential financial and health records can be gathered to invade or destroy privacy, and to facilitate widespread identity theft.

Hopelessness is exacerbated when elected political leaders betray the trust of those who put them in office. Rod Blagojevich, governor of Illinois, did so before he was indicted on nineteen counts of corruption, including offering to sell the Senate seat in his state that was vacated by President Obama and engaging in racketeering and fraud for financial gain. Likewise, the governor of

New York, Eliot Spitzer, who, despite a reputation for effectively fighting crime, was compelled to resign his office after being identified as "Client 9" in a prostitution ring. Evidence that the Bush White House approved the use of "enhanced interrogation techniques" that included torture and violated the human rights of terror suspects gravely undermined the trust of U.S. citizens in that administration.

Where do many of us turn in times of disillusionment and distrust? Some of us look to our church, synagogue, or mosque for solace, wise counsel, and role models. Catholics, however, had their trust shaken when investigations by the U.S. Attorney for Los Angeles revealed that Cardinal Roger Mahoney failed to restrict or discipline priests who had been publicly accused with convincing evidence of sexually molesting children in their parishes. Members of the Jewish faith have been troubled when heads of Jewish organizations have failed to speak out against Israeli government directives ordering troops to fire on and kill women and children in Gaza. And Muslims in the United States have been ashamed when suicide bombings perpetrated by members of their religion have killed many citizens of the Middle East.

The current worldwide leadership crisis is as great a threat to humanity as any pandemic, famine, terrorist act, or nuclear disaster—because if we fail to have courageous leadership and bold and ethical leaders, even simple solutions become impossible.

Bold Leaders

We can assure you that, in all our years of advocating for bold, unabashed leadership, we have found that leaders who truly make a difference are able to throw off despair, self-doubt, cynicism, and irresponsibility. They embrace unembarrassed optimism and unashamed enthusiasm. They are willing to speak truth to power. They assume that change is inevitable. They refuse the seduction of trying to be a self-righteous savior. Shunning greed, they look to creating value for society and the global community. They meet the gold standard for ethical leadership. They are, without a doubt, bold in their values, their commitments, and their acts of leadership.

Without ethical leadership, solutions to any problems are false, often self-serving and corrupt. Even as we admire the single leader who seems to save the day, we increasingly find that the best leaders have integrity and attract others with ethical behavior. In the collaborative mode that these leaders establish, they create stimulating, synergistic connections, support honest interactions, build trusting relationships, and encourage self-management across organizational lines. They link people through dialogue. They work with others to discover intelligent solutions and endorse viable results. They are responsible for their actions and stand by what they deliver. These leaders embody a clear commitment to values, ethics, and integrity, and yet are modest about their contributions as they enjoy the intrinsic rewards of doing good work.

Those who achieve truly unprecedented results have talent and intelligence. They have original minds. They see things differently. They spot gaps in what we know and have come to accept. They have a knack for discovering interesting, important problems and they embody the skills to solve them. They want to do the next thing, not the last one. They see connections and relationships among events and individuals. Often they combine specialized skills with broad interests and multiple frames of reference. They tend to be both deep generalists and expert specialists. They are not so immersed in any single discipline that they can't see solutions in others. They are problem seekers and solvers, and they can no more stop looking for better ways of doing things than they can give up breathing. They have flexibility as well as tenacity, which is so important in accomplishing anything of value. They are aware of what they are doing and bring their authenticity to the process.

Becoming a bold leader is intense and challenging, and to embark on it individuals must acquire a positive sense of themselves. They do so by recognizing both their abilities and their limitations. They are brave enough to solicit and integrate feedback, remain continuously open to new experiences and information, and stay attuned to the inner voice that directs them as they fulfill their promise to themselves and others.

Leaders Embrace Candor

Among the important qualities of leadership there is at least one absolute: Leaders create solutions to problems *only* when they embrace candor and signal that they are willing to listen to unpleasant truths that may be sources of data that will lead to informed decisions.

When President Barak Obama had lunch in the Oval Office with all living past-presidents (George W. Bush, Bill Clinton, George H.W. Bush, and Jimmy Carter), the *New York Times* (November 10, 2008) reported that he asked his predecessors two key questions: "How do you make sure that you get good information? How do you make sure that people aren't just telling you what you want to hear?" The soon-to-be-president was prescient regarding his need to know. Leaders rely on others to keep them informed about complex problems, and therefore they must create a climate of candor to get the information necessary to make the best decisions.

Effective leaders weigh the pertinent facts, study options, and are careful to hold their "gut reactions" in check while they are doing so. They ask powerful, challenging questions and test and judge information that may be confusing and frightening. Even when they "kick the tires" and discover information they did not want to hear, they do not shy away from evaluating what they think they know, considering all new data, and continuing their search for that nugget of knowledge that will lead to a viable solution.

Great leaders let it be known that they value candor, refusing to cater to yes-men and -women in their inner circle. They seek those who speak the truth, however hard it may be to hear. And candor goes both ways. Principled naysayers allow leaders to reevaluate their positions and learn from their mistakes. Relevant information is not merely an executive perk; leaders share it with everyone involved, whether employees in a workforce or citizens of a nation.

Good leaders make people feel that they are at the very heart of things and are counted on to contribute to the success of the enterprise. Obviously there is some information that must be kept to an inner circle, but leaders hold it to a minimum and, to the extent possible, share data that will enable their colleagues to make informed decisions and act responsibly. Those who discover they have been lied to will never trust again. Thus are enemies born.

New Definitions

The challenges that arise during times of great transition are especially daunting and call for diverse groups of talented people, committed to working together at every level of society and across every organizational hierarchy to tackle complex problems and implement coordinated, strategic solutions for the common good. The most successful leaders invite diverse minds to join them in their efforts. Consider the following shining examples: Dr. Martin Luther King Jr., Sitting Bull, Mohandas Gandhi, Cesar Chavez, Susan B. Anthony, and Nelson Mandela. One characteristic is common to these towering leaders. It is that they each had willing followers who shared their values and commitments and believed their successes were the natural outcomes of their united efforts.

Even in today's winning corporations, shared power is an everyday practice. The collaboration among the three leaders at Google, for example, accounts for much of this Internet giant's success. And when Apple's Steven Jobs temporarily stepped aside to tend to health problems, he confidently turned the role of CEO over to Tim Cook, a man he'd partnered with for eight years to lead Apple's iPod/iPhone revolution.

In government, President Obama brought this form of leadership to his administration. He demonstrated his commitment to collaborative problem solving when he appointed Republicans as cabinet members and invited his former adversary, Hillary Clinton, to be his secretary of state.

Leaders who attract willing followers to join their efforts have the talent to engage colleagues in continuous, spontaneous, creative collaboration, and results can be proudly owned, as promised by the wise Confucian scholar Lao-tzu in his *Tao Te Ching*:

> *The best of all rulers is but a shadowy presence to his subjects.*
> *Next comes the ruler they love and praise;*
> *Next comes one they fear;*
> *Next comes one with whom they take liberties....*
> *Hesitant, the best does not utter words lightly.*
> *When his task is accomplished and his work done*
> *The people all say, "it happened to us naturally."*

As we redefine leadership to meet the upheavals in our society, we must learn to lead with characteristics of powerful and effective leaders. These leaders have:

1. A Focus on Purpose, Direction, and Values

The leader's purpose is to galvanize and energize others to achieve meaningful goals. This purpose gives resonance to the work and lives of all involved. Leaders not only have a clear sense of direction, but they communicate their dream to inspire ownership by everyone in the organization. Every leader has an agenda, a set of closely held values, and a vision of "the common good." These values, the very fabric of leadership, attract us to the person whose dream we will realize.

2. A Commitment to Building Trust with Followers

Leaders generate and sustain trust, the lasting social glue that binds commitment and inspires high-quality results. To trust a leader we must have confidence that this person is competent and worth following. Our trust is inspired when leaders openly communicate and encourage dissent. Leaders generate trust by including key stakeholders to make decisions about the future.

3. A Skill in Conveying Optimism

Leaders are purveyors of hope. Their optimism communicates a belief in the worth of followers and the talents of those around them. This optimism is pervasive and powerful when leaders do not get stuck in brooding about mistakes, problems, wrong turns, or mishaps. They view errors as opportunities to learn new information, to enhance or change their dreams, to power their visions, and to redirect their strategies for achieving success. Their optimism stems from their clear vision of the future and their commitment to bringing their team along for the ride.

4. A Talent for Inspiring Action to Produce Results

Leaders have the capacity, the special knack, the talent to convert purpose and vision into actions that will produce results. Most leaders are *pragmatic* dreamers and *practical* idealists who create solutions to seemingly overwhelming problems. Moreover, they make sure they get where they want to go by living the principles they espouse. When they strive to translate ideals and intentions into reality they act ethically to make an apparent difference.

Competencies of Successful Leaders

Obviously each leader has unique skills, talents, abilities, styles, behaviors, and winning formulas. Leaders come in every race, ethnicity, age, sexual orientation, role, and circumstance imaginable. What they share, however, are six clear and powerful competencies:

- *Mastering the Context.* Leaders focus on understanding the big picture, the impact of external events on their decisions, and the forces that may be beyond their immediate control. They stand by an "internal" context of their own values, frames of reference, agendas, and ethical commitments.
- *Knowing Yourself.* Leaders deeply appreciate self-knowledge and are committed to continually learning about themselves throughout their lifetimes.

They engage in introspection and humbly solicit feedback to stimulate a lifetime of learning.

- *Creating a Vision.* Leaders create an evolving, vibrant, and compelling vision to guide their plans and mobilize others to join them in making changes. Their vision is so real that they live and breathe it.
- *Communicating with Meaning.* Leaders shape their communication by considering the concerns and intentions of their listeners. They walk in the shoes of those they wish to reach, delivering their messages to allow others to easily grasp their meaning and join in their endeavors.
- *Building Trust Through Integrity.* Leaders consistently live ethically and demonstrate their values through action. They build trust through consistency and in times of trouble can be counted on to meet challenges head-on.
- *Realizing Intentions Through Actions.* Leaders are dreamers who are skilled in producing concrete results that are expressions of their visions and values, and they consistently invite others to act with them in realizing their intentions.

Our goal in writing this book is to encourage you to develop all six of these leadership competencies. When you do so, you will be prepared for any eventuality and will be able to meet the challenges of your times with brave and brilliant leadership, as did these figures from our shared history:

Winston Churchill truly mastered the context of his shifting times, during both World Wars as well as in times of peace when he preserved the British Empire. Mother Theresa was steeped in self-knowledge as she humbly insisted that her work with the "untouchables" of India was a greater source of deep and fulfilling satisfaction for herself than for those she served. Few people can match the power of John F. Kennedy's clear vision that the United States would place a man on the moon ten years after he declared his dream. Although he did not live to see Neil Armstrong take this "giant leap for mankind," his vision resounded in that moment. A leader with legendary talent as a great communicator was Dr. Martin Luther King Jr., who moved millions to guarantee human rights for all people. What better example of a leader who lived her commitment to realizing the clear and concrete result of peace and international understanding than Eleanor Roosevelt, who united former enemies to create the United Nations? Many of us are familiar with the trust created by the integrity of the Nobel Laureate Archbishop Desmond Tutu, known as the "Rabble-Rouser for Peace." With that trust he led the unprecedented "Truth and Reconciliation Commission" in South Africa to heal his country with forgiveness and hope.

While history may not demand that we express these levels of leadership, we are certain that each of us has the capacity to become a leader in our own life. In light of this truth, we offer you an opportunity for learning and knowledge with which you can discover your innate leadership talents, hone your blunted or undiscovered skills, and express yourself as the successful leader you can be. We humbly offer the wisdom we have gleaned from others and the hope that you will value the process as much as we have enjoyed creating it. We wish you well on your journey.

Warren Bennis
University of Southern California

Joan Goldsmith
Santa Monica, California

1 A Lifetime of Learning to Lead

You better have you. The real you, the authentic examined self, not some patch-work collection of affectations and expectations, mores and mannerisms, some treadmill set to the prevailing speed of universal acceptability, the tyranny of homogeneity, whether the homogeneity of the straight world of the suits or the spiky world of the avant-garde. . . . You are only real if you can see yourself, see yourself clear and true in the mirror of your soul and smile upon the reflection. Samuel Butler once said "Life is like playing a violin solo in public, and learning the instrument as one goes on." That sounds terrifying, doesn't it, and difficult too. But that way lies music. Look in the mirror. Who is that woman? She is the work of your life; she is its greatest glory, too. Pick up your violin. Lift your bow. And play. Play your heart out.

> —**Anna Quindlen**
> **Speech to graduates, Wellesley College, delivered on May 24, 2002**

LEADERSHIP CAN BE LEARNED BY ANY OF US, NO MATTER OUR AGE, circumstances, or the challenges we face. Anna Quindlen, the successful columnist, novelist, and essayist, has it right: We *can* create ourselves, we *do* create ourselves, and the choice is ours at *each* moment and at *every* moment to learn the lessons of leadership. Unfortunately, we tend to associate learning new skills with youth, but in fact, the possibility of leading is available throughout our lifetimes; with every choice we make, we take charge of our lives. It is never too late to discover our unique voice as a leader.

Leaders are made, not born, and are created as much by themselves as by the demands of their times. They have a talent for continually learning about themselves. They seek to know who they are, what they want, why they want it, and how to gain support to achieve it. They live on the frontiers, where tomorrow is shaped. They avoid cookie-cutter patterns, come from diverse backgrounds, are of different ages and types of intelligence, have a variety of occupations and accomplishments. They are committed to continually growing throughout their lives. Some blossom only in their later years, like George Bernard Shaw, Margaret Mead, Charles Darwin, Eleanor Roosevelt, Elie Wiesel, Nelson Mandela, Mohandas Gandhi, Golda Meier, Jean Piaget, and Martha Graham. The glittering accomplishments of these great leaders demonstrate to us that it is never too late to begin.

Leaders love to learn. They continually seek exciting "aha" moments of discovery. They are questioners, probers, searchers for new ways of defining problems, and they seek innovative ways of solving them. Leaders invite partners to enhance their learning process. They engage with collaborators who see problems differently. They bravely and consistently ask for feedback from others when they err in their efforts to learn on their own. They evaluate their leadership skills and refine them, hone them, and polish them with practice. They humbly accept failure as an opportunity to rethink assumptions that led to a glitch in their efforts.

As you become a leader, you can regard the paradoxes, puzzles, and missteps that will inevitably appear as learning moments. You must take that first step. As the great hockey player Wayne Gretzky reminds us, "You miss 100 percent of the shots you *don't* take." We agree. If you fail to take the risk to act, you fail completely.

The truth is that becoming a leader is a natural expression of the life force and a highly personal journey much like that of becoming an integrated human being.

A New Approach

Programs of study, institutes, workshops, and courses that offer the study of leadership have undergone profound changes in recent years. In the bad old days, students read the biographies of charismatic "great men," who were held in awe and never questioned. In the early days of MBA programs, students were taught to revere godlike "natural" leaders who were born into their role in history. A new approach, formulated by graduate schools in the United States and adopted by European and Asian graduate schools, increasingly considers this approach irrelevant. Faculty members in the highest-ranking MBA programs openly and publicly reject the dominance of outdated teaching that leaves students ill-suited to meet the leadership demands of multinational, entrepreneurial, fast-paced organizations that are engaged in rapid and consuming demands of a chaotic world economy.

The oft-cited military model of the leader, the lone general commanding his troops, is anachronistic in a world where the ability to command and control is valued less than the ability to orchestrate, counsel, collaborate, and inspire. The recent popularity of courses that promise "instant leadership" is a symptom of our demand for a "quick fix"; such courses foster confusion about what constitutes leadership and ignore the lifetime effort it takes to learn new skills. Some people claim that leadership derives from power. Others say it stems from having a thorough and mechanistic comprehension of the nature of organizations. According to the "one-minute manager" approach, leaders emerge instantly and all that is needed is to pop Mr. or Ms. Average into a quick-action program and out pops a McLeader in sixty seconds.

In our view the only valid path to genuine leadership is one that leads to self-examination, introspection, and honest soul-searching and includes collaborative partnerships with willing colleagues. Becoming a true leader takes time and a strong commitment both to learn from failures and to make amends when necessary. Becoming a leader involves discovering your native energies and desires through self-invention and *authenticity*—being your own *author*. (The two words derive from the same Greek root.)

John Gardner, the only Republican in Lyndon Johnson's cabinet and founder of Common Cause, an advocacy organization for philanthropy, was a reticent, even shy man who nonetheless helped create innovative and durable organizations to support lasting value for the public good. He argued that the notion, endorsed by some pundits, that the attributes of a leader are innate is demonstrably false and that leadership can and must be learned. In an interview with Warren, Gardner validated our belief that if we commit to lifelong learning we will successfully become and maintain ourselves as leaders:

> No doubt certain characteristics are genetically determined—level of energy, for example. But the individual's hereditary gifts, however notable, leave the issue of future leadership performance undecided, to be settled by the later events and influences. Young people with substantial native gifts for leadership often fail to achieve what is in them to achieve. So part of our task is to develop what is naturally there but in need of cultivation. Talent is one thing; its triumphant expression is quite another. Some talents express themselves freely and with little need for encouragement. Leopold Mozart did not have to struggle to uncover buried gifts in little Wolfgang. But, generally speaking, the maturing of any complex talent requires a happy combination of motivation, character, and opportunity. Most human talent remains undeveloped.

We agree: The stakes are high and the demand for fresh, creative, risky solutions is enormous. Leaders among all citizens—of every color, ethnicity, age, and social class—are needed if we are to survive and prevail as a species. We are convinced that to lead in our own lives and make a contribution to our communities we must confront the challenging questions that currently face our society:

- Will waves of "baby boomers" struggle through the final years of their lives without adequate healthcare?

- Will our courts protect the rights of dissenters, minority populations, and the powerless to speak for themselves?
- Will private-sector leaders finally cleanse their organizations of greed and malfeasance?
- Will elected officials develop governmental regulations that create and sustain economic viability?
- Will hundreds of thousands of impoverished laid-off employees and minimum-wage workers find satisfying and useful employment?
- Will restitution be made by the banks, insurance companies, and other entities that mishandled funds and dispossessed hundreds of thousands of people from their homes, depriving them of their dreams?
- Will our children be safe from battles in distant lands, as well as from neighborhood gangs at home?
- Will our grandchildren have a world where tigers still stalk prey and glaciers are more than a memory?

It is our hope that this book will enable you to become a lifelong learner who can successfully lead efforts to find solutions to these troubling problems.

Learning How to Learn—An Exercise

As adults, we rarely have the opportunity to be true learners. Too often, we encounter low-risk, protected environments, where we choose to passively skate through someone else's requirements or go through the motions to please someone, without confronting the challenges of an authentic learning process.

When leaders lose the skill to learn, they inevitably falter and become stultified. Those who are truly committed to becoming a leader understand what it takes to learn about themselves, they honestly recognize their strengths and limitations, they solicit and integrate feedback, they stay open to new experiences, they seek diverse information, and they hear and value their own voices. Those who do so are the ones among us who will master the art of leader-as-lifelong-learner.

We advocate that you actively take risks, be self-conscious, and commit to true learning. We not only suggest that you acquire a body of knowledge about leadership but ask you to see the world as it *is* and at the same time as it *might be*, with an understanding of the distinction between the two.

Ideally, in a true learning process you will learn about *how* you learn. You will do so by paying attention to your own learning process, not just during the moments when you successfully master a new skill but also at those times when you want to give up in the face of failure. Whether you want to learn to play the piano for the first time as an adult or try bungee-jumping as a novice, you can expand your self-knowledge if you focus on understanding *how* you learn, if you listen to your inner voice as you take risks, if you observe your reactions when you are frustrated with failure, and if you discover your fears and your longings for a sense of accomplishment.

Throughout this book, we introduce activities to support your development as a leader and offer occasions for self-reflection that may reveal to you your leadership capacities. Included in these exercises are suggestions for collaboration with colleagues to enable you to tackle leadership challenges with the support of a team at work, members of your family, or friends in your community. We begin by asking you to explore the following questions.

Questions to Consider

A. Describe a challenge, new experience, or risk you took when you tried to learn something that was new and unfamiliar.

. . . .

. . . .

. . . .

. . . .

B. What were your fears before you began? How did those fears change during and after the experience? What did you learn about your fears?

. . . .

. . . .

. . . .

. . . .

C. What were your hopes and dreams as you tried to learn something new? What did you expect to discover and to achieve?

. . . .

. . . .

. . . .

. . . .

D. What did others tell you that supported or diminished your confidence when you took the risk to learn something new?

. . . .

. . . .

. . . .

. . . .

E. What people, circumstances, actions, and events supported or blocked your learning?

. . . .

. . . .

. . . .

. . . .

F. Which of your own thoughts and behaviors contributed most to your learning? Which blocked your learning?

. . . .

. . . .

. . . .

. . . .

G. At what point did you know you would be successful? What evidence do you have of your success?

. . . .

. . . .

. . . .

. . . .

H. What were the high points and payoffs of the risks you took, and what were the downsides?

. . . .

. . . .

. . . .

. . . .

I. How did your image of yourself and your thoughts about your identity change as a result of your experience?

. . . .

. . . .

. . . .

. . . .

Leaders have a hunger to learn and they know that learning leads to self-expression. They are intimately connected with *how* they learn as well as with *what* they learn. If you agree that it is worth taking the risk to learn, your next step will be to become aware of your leadership role models and to understand the impact they have had on your willingness to engage in *risky learning*.

Leadership Models—An Exercise

Our decisions about being a leader are often based on lessons we have learned from models in our families, communities, and schools as well as from distant heroes who have walked through our lives. Unconscious patterns from our past inform choices in the present and influence the view we have of ourselves. To the extent that we are unaware of these models, we fail to see the limits they impose on our leadership choices and the opportunities they offer.

Who are your friendly ghosts, the women and men who shaped your expectations and guided your aspirations to be a leader? Who were your mentors? Who walked through your dreams? Who loomed larger than life and inspired you? Who were the people who made a difference in your life?

Please consider the activities below to assist you in uncovering the models that have shaped you as a leader.

Activities to Consider

A. Name three people who walked through your dreams as leaders in your past. Write their full names, and remember who they were and how they influenced you.

. . . .

. . . .

. . . .

. . . .

B. Name three leaders whom you respect and value in your life today. Write their full names, and think about how they touch your life.

. . . .

. . . .

. . . .

. . . .

C. Consider each person you have noted and indicate the successes and failures they have had in their own lives. Make an assessment of their achievements.

. . . .

. . . .

. . . .

. . . .

. . . .

. . . .

. . . .

D. Indicate the obstacles each leader faced and overcame and the rewards they achieved by doing so.

. . . .

. . . .

. . . .

. . . .

. . . .

. . . .

. . . .

E. Assess the risks each leader took and the results that followed. Then sum up each of their lives in a few words.

. . . .

. . . .

. . . .

. . . .

. . . .

. . . .

. . . .

F. Describe how you might use the lessons you have learned from each of these leaders so that you can learn to be a more successful leader in your own life.

. . . .

. . . .

. . . .

. . . .

. . . .

. . . .

. . . .

Leadership Qualities, Attitudes, Behaviors, and Lessons—A Chart

To truly appreciate and learn from the models of leadership in your life, you must carefully analyze their life choices. Take a closer look at these models with the help of the chart below. In the first three columns, identify the *qualities*, *attitudes*, and *behaviors* of each leader. In the last column, summarize the leadership *lessons* you have learned from each leader.

For example, in the first column you might write the leader's quality of "integrity," and in the second you might list the leader's attitude as "being constructive in the face of problems." A behavior you might note in the third column is the leader's frequent "outspokenness." And in the last column you could indicate that the lesson you have drawn is to "speak your mind."

QUALITIES	ATTITUDES	BEHAVIORS	LESSONS
1.			
2.			
3.			
4.			
5.			
6.			

In the questions that follow, review your responses in the previous charts and search beneath the surface to discover not only how leaders have influenced your life but also your own leadership talents.

Questions to Consider

A. What are the positive lessons about life and leadership that you can draw from the experiences of the leaders you have identified?

. . . .

. . . .

. . . .

. . . .

. . . .

. . . .

. . . .

B. What are the negative aspects of the choices made by these women and men, and how might you avoid making the same mistakes?

. . . .

. . . .

. . . .

. . . .

. . . .

. . . .

. . . .

C. Given the qualities, attitudes, and behaviors of these leaders, what aspects of their lives have had the greatest impact on you and what did you learn from them?

. . . .

. . . .

. . . .

. . . .

. . . .

. . . .

. . . .

D. How might you thank these leaders for the influences they have had on your life? What would you like to say to them?

. . . .

. . . .

. . . .

. . . .

. . . .

. . . .

. . . .

As you complete these questions, you may want to exchange ideas with your colleagues at work or with your friends and family. The questions below will support you in creating a synthesis of your discussions with others and lead you to new insights about your leadership skills.

Questions to Consider

    A. What were the insights about leadership for each person involved in the discussion and how did they differ?

    B. If there were differences, discuss them and identify why each person held his or her views.

    C. Notice how similar qualities and messages might be interpreted by one person as positive and by another as negative. If that is the case, discuss what experiences or information created different points of view.

    D. Determine differences in qualities, attitudes, or behaviors that correspond to the positions in your organization that are held by particular leaders and also whether these differences coincide with the length of time they had on the job. If you find that hierarchical position and/or longevity had an impact on these leadership attributes, discuss why and how.

    E. If your team is part of a larger group, present a summary of your team's synthesis to the other teams and compare the similarities and differences across all teams.

You may have noticed that many of the leaders you identified were members of your family. Many of our choices are powerfully influenced by our family members, and anyone who does not master family influences will be mastered by them.

Leaders in Our Families

The family members with whom we grew up were our most powerful teachers about leadership. It was in our family that we first developed our identity, our values, our aspirations, and thus our capacities for leadership. Families powerfully influence our views of ourselves as leaders. This influence can either take the form of explicit support or be an unconscious barrier to how we demonstrate our leadership talents.

We encourage you to investigate your family's influence by discussing leadership with immediate family members. If you are fortunate enough to have older-generation relatives still living, start with them. If not, talk with siblings and cousins. If you are the sole surviving member of your family, plumb your memories or talk with childhood friends.

Questions to Consider

Who were considered leaders in your family? Who were the heroes and heroines, and what stories did you hear about leaders in past generations? What were the traits of these family members who were leaders?

Ask family members the same questions and compare their responses. Who appeared on everyone's lists? Who are the people on your list whose names did not appear on the lists of others?

LEADERS WHOM YOU IDENTIFIED   LEADERS IDENTIFIED BY OTHERS

. . . .

. . . .

. . . .

. . . .

. . . .

. . . .

. . . .

A. How did your family view leadership? Was leadership considered to be something in the distance that only "great men" achieved? Did your family value leaders of both genders and of various age groups?

. . . .

. . . .

. . . .

. . . .

. . . .

. . . .

. . . .

B. In what respects was leadership defined differently for each gender or age group in your family?

. . . .

. . . .

. . . .

. . . .

. . . .

. . . .

. . . .

C. Were leaders identified in terms of a particular role, a particular place in the sibling hierarchy, or a special branch of the family? If so, how?

. . . .

. . . .

. . . .

. . . .

. . . .

. . . .

. . . .

D. What signals were sent to you by your family about being a leader? Who sent them, and how were they delivered? Was the communication about leaders subtle or direct?

. . . .

. . . .

. . . .

. . . .

. . . .

. . . .

. . . .

E. What were your family's expectations about the leadership of people who differed in race, ethnicity, age, gender, sexual orientation, or disability?

. . . .

. . . .

. . . .

. . . .

. . . .

. . . .

. . . .

F. How did your family encourage or discourage you with respect to exercising leadership skills, and what decisions did you make based on their expectations?

. . . .

. . . .

. . . .

. . . .

. . . .

. . . .

. . . .

After analyzing your family's views of leadership, compare your thoughts with those of people at work, in school, or in your community. As you exchange anecdotes and diverse responses, you may notice common themes, insights, and conclusions. You may also find varying attitudes toward leadership in different families. Look for ways in which gender, culture, religion, race, ethnicity, immigration, and social class have influenced leadership expectations and patterns in the families you compare.

In this exercise, we hope that you have discovered what shaped your personal views of leadership and that you have gained a perspective regarding the leaders whom you valued and their influences on the decisions you have made. The observations from others may clarify your family's contribution to your views of yourself as a leader.

Organizational Leaders—A Chart

Family leadership patterns certainly influence us on our jobs, and they are re-shaped and revised by the values, culture, and expectations of the organizations where we work. We learn about leadership from colleagues and take messages from the structures, systems, and demands of our jobs.

Take a dispassionate look at your workplace and notice how you are influenced by the place where you spend the majority of your waking hours. How are leaders viewed, and what are the ways they are developed and rewarded? How are they discouraged, ignored, or punished? What has been the impact of these implicit and explicit messages of your organization on your views of yourself as a leader?

As you view leadership in your chart below, you may see the ways your organization supports leadership with awards, promotions, and acknowledgments or with subtler inducements such as invitations to training programs and social events, access to confidential communications, prime office or worksite locations, additional vacation time, and humane treatment in times of stress.

In the chart below, please indicate hidden as well as explicit messages that support or suppress leadership development.

MY ORGANIZATION SUPPORTS LEADERSHIP BY:	MY ORGANIZATION OBSTRUCTS LEADERSHIP BY:
. . . .	. . . .
. . . .	. . . .
. . . .	. . . .
. . . .	. . . .
. . . .	. . . .
. . . .	. . . .
. . . .	. . . .

After completing the chart, draw your conclusions regarding the implicit and explicit ways that your organization supports or blocks leadership development.

Conclusions

. . . .

. . . .

. . . .

. . . .

. . . .

. . . .

. . . .

You may want to share your conclusions with colleagues or friends who know about your organization. If you do, ask them for their feedback. If you are part of a team, ask the members to complete the chart and then discuss their results.

Activities to Consider

    A. Compare team members' charts and discuss differences and commonalities.

    B. Discuss specific examples of situations each person has experienced that have supported or obstructed their leadership at work.

    C. See if everyone can agree on those aspects of your organization that support or obstruct leadership. Complete a chart that shows the agreements you have reached, and decide whether you want to share the conclusions of your team with other teams in your organization and discuss common factors and underlying dynamics.

As you examine leadership messages in your organization, consider how your work experience has influenced your choices about being a leader and judge whether you have gained self-respect as a result of your work experience. If you adopt the leadership qualities of those you admire in your organization you may expand your self-respect as a leader. Novelist and essayist Joan Didion, in what has now become the classic collection of her essays, *Slouching Towards Bethlehem*, reflects on self-respect:

> Self-respect is a discipline, a habit of mind that can never be faked but can be developed, trained, coaxed forth. . . . To free us from the expectations of others, to give us back to ourselves—there lies the great, the singular power of self-respect.

We add to Didion's reflection that self-respect, like other leadership qualities, can be learned, and can flow not only from freeing ourselves from the expectations of others but also from our expectations of ourselves that have been influenced by unseen myths about leadership.

Leadership Myths—An Exercise

Myths about leaders may present barriers to learning to be a leader if you unquestionably accept them as true. If we unconsciously believe them, we may negatively shape our beliefs about ourselves and limit our access to leadership.

There are five myths in particular that you must disabuse if you are to become a powerful and successful leader. We invite you to recall when you first heard them, experienced them, or bought into them as your own. With insights about these myths and their influence, you may notice the price you paid by believing in them and understand their hidden and constrictive power.

1. Leadership Is a Rare and Unusual Talent

Nothing could be further from the truth. While great leaders may be as rare as great runners, actors, or painters, we are convinced that everyone has the potential to be a leader. There are millions of leaders throughout the world, distinguished by their ability to seize the moment, rise to the challenge, and make committed efforts to save the day.

When have you accepted this myth, and who first suggested it or currently perpetuates it?

. . . .

. . . .

. . . .

. . . .

What price have you paid for accepting or rejecting this myth?

. . . .

. . . .

. . . .

. . . .

2. Leaders Are Born, and Only to Elite Families, Races, Castes, or Social Classes

Biographies of great leaders sometimes read as if these individuals entered the world with extraordinary genetic endowments. The truth is that the major capacities for leadership can be learned, if the will and the desire for learning them are there. Becoming a leader is a deeply human process, full of trial and error, victory and defeat, timing and happenstance, intuition and insight, and available to all people, everywhere and at every time.

When have you accepted this myth, and who first suggested it or currently perpetuates it?

. . . .

. . . .

. . . .

. . . .

What price have you paid for accepting or rejecting this myth?

. . . .

. . . .

. . . .

. . . .

3. Leaders Are Always Charismatic

Some are, but most successful leaders show signs of hesitancy, insecurity, and doubt, appearing "all too human" and stumbling from time to time. Charisma is one of the *results* of powerful leadership. Those who master leadership attributes are granted respect, even awe, by followers who then point to charisma as one of their defining qualities when praising them.

When have you accepted this myth, and who first suggested it or currently perpetuates it?

. . . .

. . . .

. . . .

. . . .

What price have you paid for accepting or rejecting this myth?

. . . .

. . . .

. . . .

. . . .

4. Leadership Can Be Found Only at the *Top* of an Organization

It is obviously a mistake to limit our search for leaders to only the executives at the top of large organizations. In fact, leaders can be found and supported in labor unions, staff forums, self-directed work teams, day-to-day efforts at quality, and informal projects located at the bottom of organizational hierarchies and on every level in between.

When have you accepted this myth, and who first suggested it or currently perpetuates it?

. . . .

. . . .

. . . .

. . . .

What price have you paid for accepting or rejecting this myth?

. . . .

. . . .

. . . .

. . . .

5. The Leader Controls, Directs, Prods, and Manipulates Others

This is perhaps the most dangerous myth of all. On the contrary, leaders have visions that they communicate to attract and pull others to join their endeavors. They understand they will not be successful if they try to push or coerce would-be followers. True leaders enable any followers they may have to take their *own* initiative in solving shared problems.

When have you accepted this myth, and who first suggested it or currently perpetuates it?

. . . .

. . . .

. . . .

. . . .

What price have you paid for accepting or rejecting this myth?

. . . .

. . . .

. . . .

. . . .

6. Other Myths

Can you think of other myths, misconceptions, and stereotypes about leadership that you have encountered or chosen to believe? If you are working in a team, create a list of the myths that are in your organization and discuss how they have influenced your team and prevented leaders from emerging.

What are some additional myths about leadership in your organization?

. . . .

. . . .

. . . .

. . . .

How have you and others accepted or rejected these myths or influenced others to accept them?

. . . .

. . . .

. . . .

. . . .

When myths about leadership become obvious and explicit, we can readily see their impact on individuals and organizations. Thus executives and staff can be liberated from the toxic power of destructive myths. As you analyze leadership myths that are active in your organization, share your insights with colleagues to gain their support in overcoming these myths and freely choose your expressions of leadership. If you consider the following questions you will not only transform yourself as a leader but will create a more empowering culture for your organization.

Questions to Consider

A. Identify individuals who are examples of each leadership myth in your organization, and state the purpose each myth serves. What establishes each myth and who perpetuates it?

. . . .

. . . .

. . . .

. . . .

. . . .

. . . .

. . . .

B. What are the most toxic myths about leaders in your organization? How does the organization propagate these leadership myths and communicate them to newcomers, to clients or customers, and to everyone at all levels of the hierarchy?

. . . .

. . . .

. . . .

. . . .

. . . .

. . . .

. . . .

C. How have these leadership myths influenced your behavior and your self-image as a leader in your organization?

. . . .

. . . .

. . . .

. . . .

. . . .

. . . .

. . . .

D. What interests have been served in your organization by maintaining each myth? What are the hidden agendas for advocating each myth, and who has bought into it or rejected it?

. . . .

. . . .

. . . .

. . . .

. . . .

. . . .

. . . .

We have raised the specter of overpowering and pervasive myths about leadership to sound an alarm and to lessen any power they have over your views of yourself as a leader. To transform yourself into a more effective leader, you must consider these myths as breakers, not makers; traps, not launching pads; and ends, not beginnings, of learning to lead. Unique and authentic definitions of leadership skills await you as you act on your insights and instincts. Leaders have no mandate other than the one they hear from their own voice, which urges them to take a stand for what they believe. We support you in finding that voice and adhering to its commands to demonstrate audacious leadership!

2 Audacious Leadership

I remember when I became the first woman and the first African American President at the University of Michigan Dearborn campus someone said that African Americans and women could see me as a role model. And another colleague said that what is more important is for white young men and women to see an African American woman in a position like this and to see her as successful. It changes the way everyone looks at opportunity. I see leadership as giving people a way of thinking about the future—leadership is about hope and the audacity of hope, it truly is.

—Dr. Blenda Wilson
"New Horizons!" *Los Angeles Times*, **January 19, 2009**

THE CONSTANCY OF CHANGE THAT DRIVES EFFORTS TO REINVENT government bureaucracies, church hierarchies, and business practices calls for audacious leaders who take a stand for what they believe in. These leaders avoid the dangerous addiction to power that is based on ambition. They counterbalance toxic ambition with competence and integrity. These three qualities comprise a three-legged stool on which true leadership sits. Competence, ambition, and integrity must be in balance for leadership to be constructive as an audacious force.

If this triad shifts out of balance, three negative outcomes result. The unfortunate combination of ambition and competence without integrity leaves us with self-serving leaders who place personal power above ethics, and self-interest before the good of the whole. The seemingly attractive combination of integrity and ambition without competence leaves us with well-meaning leaders who are unable to realize promised results and thus take followers to a righteous dead end. And integrity paired with competence may appear to be enviable and lead to good works, but if ambition is missing leaders fail to risk challenging the status quo or opening new ground. A three-way balance, by contrast, allows leaders to be ethically true to the integrity of their vision and to humbly and collaboratively make that vision challenging and real for others. Audacious leaders make a sacred trust with followers to honor a powerful partnership that will build joint endeavors to meet the expressed needs of all concerned.

The awesome responsibility of finding the right path for those who trust them requires leaders to be in touch with the real world and to avoid getting lost in fantasies of omnipotence. True leaders continually ask questions, probe for information, test their own perceptions, and recheck the facts. They talk to their constituents. They want to know, and are committed to finding out, what their potential adversaries are thinking. They search for better ideas. They want to know what's working and what is not. They keep an open mind and invite serendipity to bring them the fresh knowledge they crave.

Leaders Are Distinct from Managers

There is a call, at the beginning of this tumultuous twenty-first century, for a new brand of leaders who are distinct from what we think of as traditional managers.

Whereas managers are necessary to keep the machinery oiled and the organization on track, leaders are crucial to create a viable future, empower others to make it real, foster continual learning and growth, and enable those traditional managers to get their jobs done, and done well. This distinction between leaders and managers is vital to understanding what it will take to meet the demands of our times and to provide for the roles that will successfully deliver the future we need and want. Leaders master and alter the context—the turbulent, ambiguous surroundings that seem to conspire against them and threaten to suffocate them. Managers surrender to the context, without challenging it. They are focused on commanding others and controlling the details. Leaders investigate reality, embracing and carefully analyzing the pertinent factors. On the basis of their investigations, they actively dream up and powerfully communicate visions, concepts, plans, and programs. Managers are more likely to accept what others tell them and to take it for granted as the truth. They implement visions without probing for a deeper understanding of what is truly needed or wanted and why that is so. Leading is about effectiveness. Managing is about efficiency. Leading is about direction and values, about what and why. Management is about systems, controls, procedures, policies, and structures. Leadership is about trusting people to innovate and initiate. Management is about copying and maintaining the status quo. Leadership is about being creative and adaptive; it is about searching the horizon, not just considering the bottom line. And, in fact, every organization needs and wants both roles to be filled by appropriate candidates who understand the expectations for their roles and are committed to getting the job done. In short, there is a profound difference—a chasm—between leaders and managers. To state it succinctly: *A manager does things right. A leader does the right things.*

Doing the right things implies knowing what is right, having a clear sense of values and goals, committing to a direction, an objective, a vision, a dream, a path, a reach. It requires remaining true to an overarching integrity. *Doing things right* implies focusing attention on following directions and meeting standards that have been specified by someone who is perceived to have power and must be obeyed. Leaders base their appeal to others on their integrity, on a careful estimate of the forces at play, and on trends and contradictions in competing conclusions. They are able to create a compelling vision that takes others to a new place, and when they enroll others in this vision, they inspire them and empower them to accomplish good deeds. They pull rather than push by attracting and inviting others to identify with the task and the goal.

In a lecture not long ago, as Warren was discussing the ability of leaders to attract others, a woman in the audience said, "I have a deaf daughter, so I've learned American Sign Language and found this to be the sign for the word 'manage.'" She held out her hands as if she were holding the reins of a horse, or restraining someone from reacting. She went on, "The sign for 'lead' is like this." She cradled her arms and rocked back and forth the way a parent would lovingly hold a child. We could not have said it better and suggest this image to make the distinction clear.

All organizations must have both managers and leaders to succeed. However, the old managerial structures and systems that exalted control, order, and predictability and demanded that all managers limit themselves to following precedent or current rules are increasingly giving way to democratic structures and systems that exalt innovation, creativity, and rapid response, thus requiring the presence of leaders at all levels of the organization.

In this new way of doing things, creativity, diversity, and dissent are encouraged over blind loyalty, and leaders function as facilitators rather than as autocrats—as appreciators of ideas rather than as defenders of them. While managers accomplish specific, concrete goals, leaders identify the goals in the first place, and rally support to achieve them.

No organization can function successfully if either of these roles remains unfilled, yet there is a danger of confusing them, of failing to provide for both, and of diminishing the contribution of each. Trust and respectful collaboration between leaders and managers are prized in successful organizations where these roles inform each other. This chart clarifies the distinctions between leader and manager and provides a clear picture so you can fully understand the requirements for success in either role:

Chart of Distinctions Between Manager and Leader

The manager administers; the leader innovates.
The manager is a copy; the leader is an original.
The manager maintains; the leader develops.

The manager accepts reality; the leader investigates it.

The manager focuses on systems and structure; the leader focuses on people.

The manager relies on control; the leader inspires trust.

The manager has a short-range view; the leader has a long-range perspective.

The manager asks how and when; the leader asks what and why.

The manager has her eye always on the bottom line; the leader has her eye on the horizon.

The manager imitates; the leader originates.

The manager accepts the status quo; the leader challenges it.

The manager is the classic good soldier; the leader is her own person.

The manager does things right; the leader does the right thing.

Bringing the Distinction Home—An Exercise

The distinctions between manager and leader pose a very clear challenge to you. Can you apply these distinctions to your work, community, and home environments? Can you observe yourself carefully on your job, in your community, and even in your family to see if you are acting to control and manage others? Or are you seeking to empower and lead them? Is your first reaction when you are faced with a problem to react as a manager and merely "follow the rules"? Or are you willing to discover what is right for yourself and all the others involved? In this exercise you will have the opportunity to consider these questions and to understand how making the distinctions between manager and leader can enable you to become an audacious leader.

In the space below, we ask you to identify the leaders and managers in your organization, school, nonprofit, social group, and family. Begin by making two lists. In the first, note the names and positions of the leaders whom you can identify, and in the second, list the names and positions of the managers in your life.

Examples of Leaders

NAME   POSITION

1. . . . .

2. . . . .

3. . . . .

4. . . . .

5. . . . .

6. . . . .

7. . . . .

8. . . . .

Examples of Managers

NAME   POSITION

1. . . . .

2. . . . .

3. . . . .

4. . . . .

5. . . . .

6. . . . .

7. . . . .

8. . . . .

Questions to Consider

A. Read through the names of the managers and leaders you have listed above. Do you notice any distinctions between them other than the ones we mentioned in the

Chart of Distinctions Between Manager and Leader? If you find additional distinctions, include them on the chart.

B. Place yourself in this picture by adding your name to the appropriate list, as a leader or manager or both.

C. Was it easier to identify managers or leaders? If so, which ones? And how do you explain the difference?

. . . .

. . . .

. . . .

. . . .

D. Did you include more people in one category than in the other? If so, which one and why?

. . . .

. . . .

. . . .

. . . .

E. Do the members of your organization or group tend to value and support managers or leaders to a greater extent? If so, how do they display favoritism? How does their doing so detract from the organization or contribute to it?

. . . .

. . . .

. . . .

. . . .

F. Describe the ways in which your organization, family, or community encourages or discourages leaders from acting and developing.

. . . .

. . . .

. . . .

. . . .

G. Where did you place yourself on the list, and why? Ask your colleagues or friends if they agree with your choice.

. . . .

. . . .

. . . .

. . . .

Now that you have completed this exercise, you may find that you've discovered some new perceptions about yourself. With your new insights, take this opportunity to learn from your colleagues and engage in collaborative learning. If you can organize small-group discussions, you will have the chance to test your perceptions and participate in some give-and-take. By doing so, you will clarify your ideas and learn from the diversity of opinions that emerge. Take the time to find a partner or a team of associates with whom you can share your ideas and further develop your understanding of leadership.

Activities to Consider

A. Present your revised *Chart of Distinctions Between Manager and Leader* to your companions and see if everyone agrees about which distinctions are relevant to you. If you find differences, discuss them until you reach a consensus, or recognize multiple truths.

B. Discuss the managers and leaders on each person's list in round-robin fashion, and ask each person to share his or her list and any additional distinctions that come to mind. Discuss the similarities and differences in your views of leadership skills.

C. Explain where you placed yourself in the list. Ask your colleagues if they agree with how you saw yourself. Each group member should then give the others feedback in the same way.

D. If you have access to other teams who are discussing the *Chart of Distinctions Between Manager and Leader*, share your chart with others and revise and integrate everyone's list to represent all the teams.

E. Finally, come to a consensus regarding the characteristic skills of managers and leaders in your organization and brainstorm how to support courageous leadership among your colleagues.

Leaders Build Trust Through Integrity

Interest in leadership surged after the attacks on the World Trade Center in New York on September 11, 2001, and continued to increase as a result of the tragic, almost unstoppable violence in the Middle East and the ballooning world economic crisis. Accordingly, there is an urgent need for a critical mass of citizens in the informal sector to make a great evolutionary leap to become audacious leaders.

If we review the causes of today's financial crisis, we find many managers who were motivated by greed rather than by integrity or a commitment to protect the common good. Yet a number of courageous leaders emerged as well. One was Marcel Ospel, the former chairman of UBS Bank in Zurich, Switzerland. At his urging, two of his colleagues joined him in relinquishing 33 million Swiss francs (equivalent to 29 million U.S. dollars) in salary; they also returned their bonuses to their bank, and partly as a result of their selfless action, the Swiss government rescued this bank. It survived and was able to continue paying living wages to its workforce.

In contrast to Marcel Ospel, some leaders who do the right thing are not recognized in their lifetimes. One such leader was Adolf Merckle, a German businessman whose body was discovered on the railroad tracks near his home. Merckle's huge debts and complicated financial transactions ended with the failure of the firm he had founded thirty-four years earlier. Fearing the loss of jobs for 12,000 employees, he took his own life, not realizing that his efforts to prevent bankruptcy had actually succeeded. The day after his suicide, his firm was sold. His leadership saved all of his workers' jobs and protected the livelihoods of the other businesses in his hometown. An overflowing crowd attended his funeral, where he was lauded as a decent leader who looked after his employees and actively contributed to his community. Though ranked No. 94 on *Forbes'* list of the world's 100 richest people, he never distanced himself from the human concerns of those who worked for him. The stories of both Ospel and Merckle remind us that when leaders are personally committed to doing the right thing, even in the hardest times they can make a significant difference.

As students of the vast, amorphous, slippery, and desperately important subject of leadership, we know full well that some leaders turn out to be dangerous, unsavory, even *toxic*. Our longtime friend and associate Jean Lipman-Blumen, a professor at Claremont University's Peter Drucker School of Management, has described these profoundly dangerous individuals in her book *The Allure of Toxic Leaders*, where she undertakes the daunting task of analyzing what makes bad leaders tick and, more important, why we *choose* them. In an e-mail conversation in the spring of 2009, Jean expanded her analysis of our attraction to toxic, perverse leaders:

> Yes, I do think the basic driver that propels us into the arms of toxic leaders is existential anxiety stemming from the certainty of death and the uncertainty of the particular circumstances under which it will occur. So, we

succumb to the leader's (savior's) illusions of safety and certainty. Moreover, it is not just our physical death but the fear of having the memory of our very existence wiped clean from the societal ledger that drives us to find ways to become heroic. That is a major reason why the illusions of toxic leaders become so seductive, offering, as they do, a path to heroism and immortality. (Napoleon said immortality was merely memory in the minds of other people.)

This existential anxiety is the most compelling explanation for why we succumb to toxic leaders, and it is buttressed by other important psychological needs: our need for authority figures to replace our parents; our yearning to feel chosen and special; our longing to be part of the human community and its opposite, the fear of ostracism, isolation, and social death; and our sense of impotence when we consider confronting and rejecting a toxic leader.

Our basic fear is reinforced by the sociological circumstances (e.g., crises, culture, unraveling knowledge, change and ambiguity, destructive social norms and the toxic institutions these leaders create) in which we inevitably live, with each historical moment adding its own unique challenges. Existential anxiety is the most fundamental reason and it is anchored by a host of other psychological and sociological factors. When I begin to think of this topic again, I wonder how any of us can hope to resist toxic leaders, particularly when their illusions come wrapped in charisma.

We are grateful for Jean's powerful warning. In these times that threaten destructive chaos, it serves as an antidote to those with charisma who offer simplistic solutions and seek our blind trust.

The premise of this book is that, even in difficult circumstances, natural leaders will emerge on every level of society and right any wrongs that have been perpetrated. They will automatically build trust, and when they do so they will exhibit four character traits that we can recognize and adopt.

First, and most important, leaders have the *competency* to do an excellent job. Skill in performing required tasks as well as the ability to mentor and coach others are the initial measures that successful leaders take. Second, leaders have *congruity*; they are known for being persons of integrity, with values that match their actions. Effective leaders make sure that what they espouse is congruent with what they do. Third, leaders have *constancy* so that their followers believe that they are on their side in the heat of battle and will come through for them to overcome problems. Finally, leaders are *caring*. They are trusted to be genuinely concerned about the lives of the people they touch, and they empathize and are responsible for the results of their decisions.

Applying Leadership Skills—An Exercise

No one need be solely a leader or a manager in all circumstances. In fact, a continuum exists between the two roles; in some instances you will behave more as a leader and in others more as a manager. In the following activity we ask you to place yourself on this continuum between leader and manager. As you do so, keep in mind that you may demonstrate one role or the other at different times and under different circumstances. Also notice certain thinking styles and types of behaviors you may want to develop that will enable you to take more of a leadership approach to the problems you face.

Tables 1 through 4 below ask you to contrast five aspects of managing and leading: *character traits*, *functions*, *philosophies*, and *expected results*. On the left side of each table you will find characteristics commonly associated with managing; and on the right side, those that are associated with leading. Between the two poles is a scale from 1 to 5: Here, you will circle the number that best indicates the thoughts and behaviors you most often exhibit.

The Leadership Inventory

Table 1:   Character Traits: Leading and Managing

	Managing	Your Assessment	Leading
Seeks situations of	Stability	1 2 3 4 5	Change
	Prosperity	1 2 3 4 5	Uncertainty
Focuses on goals of	Continuity	1 2 3 4 5	Improvement
	Optimization of resources	1 2 3 4 5	Innovation
Bases power on	Position of authority	1 2 3 4 5	Personal influence
Demonstrates skills in	Technical competence	1 2 3 4 5	Diagnosis and conceptualization
	Supervision	1 2 3 4 5	Persuasion
	Administration	1 2 3 4 5	Dealing with ambiguity
Works toward outcome of	Employee compliance	1 2 3 4 5	Employee commitment

Table 2:   Functions: Leading and Managing

	Managing	Your Assessment	Leading
Planning strengths	Tactics	1 2 3 4 5	Strategy
	Logistics	1 2 3 4 5	Policy formation
	Focus on details	1 2 3 4 5	Seeing the big picture
Staffing approach	Selection based on qualifications	1 2 3 4 5	Developing shared values
Directing methods	Clarifying objectives	1 2 3 4 5	Coaching
	Coordinating	1 2 3 4 5	Role modeling
	Establishing reward systems	1 2 3 4 5	Inspiring
Controlling methods	Standard operating procedures	1 2 3 4 5	Motivation
	Monitoring	1 2 3 4 5	Self-management
Performance evaluation approach	Rewards discipline	1 2 3 4 5	Support development
Decision-making qualities	Analytical	1 2 3 4 5	Intuitive
	Risk-averse	1 2 3 4 5	Risk-taking
	Rational	1 2 3 4 5	Ambiguous
Communication style	Transactional	1 2 3 4 5	Transformational
	Top-down	1 2 3 4 5	Persuasive

Table 3: Philosophies: Leading and Managing

	Managing	Your Assessment	Leading
Oriented toward	Programs & procedures	1 2 3 4 5	People & concepts
Resources valued	Physical	1 2 3 4 5	People
	Fiscal & technical	1 2 3 4 5	Knowledge-based
Information base of	Data, facts	1 2 3 4 5	Feelings, emotions, & ideas
	Precedent	1 2 3 4 5	Things to learn
Human resources as	Assets to meet current organizational needs	1 2 3 4 5	Corporate resources for future developments
Change attitude	Implements change when directed	1 2 3 4 5	Sees change as a raison d'être

Table 4: Expected Results: Leading and Managing

	Managing	Your Assessment	Leading
Defines success as	Maintenance of quality	1 2 3 4 5	Employee commitment
	Stability & consistency	1 2 3 4 5	Mutuality/trust
	Efficiency	1 2 3 4 5	Effectiveness
Does not want to experience	Anarchy	1 2 3 4 5	Inertia
	Employee disorientation	1 2 3 4 5	Lack of motivation
	Surprises	1 2 3 4 5	Boredom
Is unsuccessful when experiencing	Deviation from authority	1 2 3 4 5	Wrong direction/vision
	Employee resistance	1 2 3 4 5	Failure to communicate vision
	Low performance	1 2 3 4 5	Lack of buy-in

Now that you have completed this inventory, review your responses to each item and notice any patterns that emerge. Are there areas you want to change so that you can be more of a leader? And did you find the continuum incomplete in its range of options? If so, please make changes in the chart to add new choices.

If you are able to share your assessment with an associate, ask for feedback about your perceptions and note any similarities and differences between your views and those of your colleague.

Creating Your Personal Leadership Agenda—An Exercise

Now take another look at *The Leadership Inventory* and notice any traits you circled to be a 3 or below. These traits can be placed on your *Personal Leadership Agenda*, and you may address them as you continue to learn to lead.

In the exercise below, you will identify specific *behaviors* you want to change to be more of a leader, the *supports* that might assist you, and the *barriers* that may inhibit you from being an audacious leader. When you consider the supports and barriers to your becoming a leader, remember that in any change effort there will always be people and circumstances that can enable you in being a leader and others that will block your success.

Personal Leadership Agenda

BEHAVIORS I WISH TO CHANGE	SUPPORTS	BARRIERS
1.		

. . . .

. . . .

. . . .

. . . .

. . . .

2.

. . . .

. . . .

. . . .

. . . .

. . . .

3.

. . . .

. . . .

. . . .

. . . .

. . . .

4.

. . . .

. . . .

. . . .

. . . .

. . . .

5.

. . . .

. . . .

. . . .

. . . .

. . . .

6.

. . . .

. . . .

. . . .

. . . .

. . . .

7.

. . . .

. . . .

. . . .

. . . .

. . . .

8.

. . . .

. . . .

. . . .

. . . .

. . . .

9.

. . . .

. . . .

. . . .

. . . .

. . . .

10.

. . . .

. . . .

. . . .

. . . .

. . . .

When you have completed drafting your agenda, you may want to share it with colleagues and ask for their feedback as well as for their support in your development as a leader. If your friends have completed a similar agenda, compare results, give them feedback, and offer your support for *their* leadership development. Look for features that you all have in common, features that may indicate hidden dynamics and expectations in your organization, community, or family that reinforce certain behaviors and restrict others. Your awareness of these aspects of the environment will allow you to counter barriers and take advantage of opportunities for success.

Now that you have an agenda for developing yourself as a leader, you are prepared to learn the six competencies of leaders. As you do so, we invite you to become an audacious leader that this world so urgently needs. Are you ready to begin? Let's get started.

3 Mastering the Context:
Competency One

We must make . . . an emergency rescue of human civilization from the imminent and rapidly growing threat posed by the climate crisis. The electrifying redemption of America's revolutionary declaration that all human beings are born equal sets the stage for the renewal of U.S. leadership in a world that desperately needs to protect its primary endowment: the integrity and livability of the planet. . . .

Here is the good news: The bold steps that are needed to solve the climate crisis are exactly the same steps that ought to be taken in order to solve the economic crisis and the energy security crisis.

—**Al Gore**
"Global Warming I: The Climate for Change," *New York Times,*
November 10, 2008

THERE IS PROBABLY NO MORE IMPORTANT CONTEXT FOR LEADERS TO master than that of the global environment. Without a formal position in any government, university, or laboratory and lacking any designated authority for mandating solutions, former Vice President Al Gore is nonetheless a leader in actively addressing the dangers of global warming. We are pleased to note that, as a result of his efforts to save the environment, he has been awarded the Nobel Peace Prize.

Gore's urgency in moving quickly on policies and actions to stem destructive climate change reminds us that leaders are conscious of, knowledgeable about, and willing to take on challenges posed by the external context of world forces, scientific discoveries, and theoretical trends. Effective leaders of our times are also conscious of, engaged with, and guided by an internal context that encompasses values, political and religious beliefs, theoretical frameworks, and intellectual commitments that motivate them to take an ethical stand and act to make necessary changes. Gore demonstrated mastery of both the external and the internal contexts when he took a leadership role in linking efforts to save the U.S. economy to long-term initiatives to save the planet and vice versa. As he noted, major technological innovations, investment opportunities, greenhouse-gas reduction, and financial returns result when low-emission power plants and energy-efficient factories are built and environmentally safe products are developed.

The term "context" refers to the larger environment in which we live and work—specifically, the culture of our organizations as well as the political, social, and economic realities that shape our lives. When we perceive the elements of the *big-picture context* and understand the forces and opportunities inherent in it, we can be responsible leaders who can shape our time and place in history.

In fact, each of us has an *internal context*, comprised of our values, political, social and religious beliefs, and our intellectual commitments that guide us to solutions for the problems we face. Skill in mastering both the external and internal contexts matters today as it has never mattered before.

Over the past millennia, there have been leaders who perceived and understood the seemingly daunting forces that overwhelmed humanity. With their understanding they confronted threatening contexts and righted the wrongs of their times. Whenever we face difficult times on the world stage or at home, questions about the larger context must be addressed if we are to lessen their impact. Following are some of the big-picture questions we must try to answer in today's world:

- Will a large portion of our population struggle through our final years without a social services safety net that allows us to feel secure?
- Are the drugs we take and the food and water we consume healthy and safe, or will they cause future threats to our health?
- Will our children be educated to succeed, or will our public schools slide into mediocrity and disaster?
- Will our courts protect the right of minorities, immigrants, and the powerless, or will they be biased against those of us who most need justice?
- Will our grandchildren survive environmental changes that permanently threaten our planet?

These problems and many others may seem daunting even for the most talented of leaders. But those who master the big-picture context and mobilize their internal context will have the skills to meet these challenges and more.

Confronting Contextual Challenges

To find the solutions to such problems, you must identify and analyze the threats posed by external forces and also ground yourself in your inner values. In the pages that follow, we will ask you to consider several big-picture contextual issues requiring your leadership, and these issues require that you enhance your skills in applying your internal context as a more powerful leader.

1. Demographic Changes

Demographic changes challenge the stability of every society. Not only is the global population increasing rapidly but the sixty-and-older crowd is living longer and healthier. In the 1960s, according to the journal *Economist*, men could expect to spend fifty of their sixty-eight years of life expectancy in paid work. Today, they are likely to work for only thirty-eight of their seventy-six years. Organizations are searching for ways to retain the wisdom of their aging employees without sidelining or ignoring coming generations. The social and public policy issues raised by these and other shifting demographics have serious implications. Let's consider just one: If workers continue to take early retirement (and the average age of retirement seems to be approaching the early sixties in the United States and lower in European countries), and with "baby boomers" in massive numbers hitting retirement age, the number of wage earners will be too small to support social security or provide for other social programs for boomer retirees.

A visible demographic change that has triggered violence and created grave divisions is the burgeoning immigrant population in North America and Western Europe. On the one hand, highly educated and technically skilled immigrants are being welcomed and even recruited by the hi-tech industries of the United States, Canada, the United Kingdom, and Western Europe. On the other hand, unskilled and uneducated immigrants are crossing borders and traversing dangerous seas to reach the North and being herded into camps with reportedly unlivable conditions. Some are arrested and exported back to their countries of origin to face not just grueling conditions but further arrests or death.

2. Social Contracts

Social contracts between employers and employees are increasingly being blown apart. Those hallowed implicit contracts that offered loyalty and responsibility to both parties have been lost in the turbulence of economic crisis. Roughly 25 percent of the U.S. workforce was dumped between 1985 and 2005, and at present that number is growing monthly by millions of laid-off employees and furloughed civil servants. Union members can no longer rely on labor contracts to protect their jobs or retirement packages, and a recent survey reported in the *Wall Street Journal* revealed that even those employees who have a job stay less than three years. We calculate that the churn of the workforce—that is, the number of workers who are temporarily out of work or who are looking for new opportunities at any given moment—amounts to 30–35 percent of the workforce. In short, during this first decade of the twenty-first century, leaders are being challenged to reduce the impact of nascent, potentially disruptive economic forces.

3. Modern Technologies

Modern technologies have created mixed results: isolated enclaves of people who retreat into their own electronic castles, on the one hand, and powerful links bringing people together, on the other. Many of us face daily, instant choices as to how and when to activate technology and which modes to choose. Employees are increasingly working at home and communicating with the world via computers that screen their calls, find movies for their VCRs and DVDs, order takeout food for their microwave ovens, and offer indoor exercises to keep their bodies in shape. Students are increasingly turning to online courses, virtual seminars, and discussion groups for college credits and advanced degrees. What once were communities of learners have become isolated, "self-guided," hermetically sealed worlds. Workers or students in these environments retreat into virtual worlds and digital second lives. Trend-spotters call this phenomenon "cocooning," but it looks to us more like social isolation.

On the other hand, these same technologies have linked distant family members and new and old friends, resulting in satisfying relationships and even love affairs. They also allow psychotherapists, coaches, organizational consultants, mediators, and other professionals to maintain their practices with clients and patients across long distances. Facebook, MySpace, YouTube, Skype, and other linking devices allow for instant contact among networks of individuals who might otherwise remain isolated from one another.

4. Social, Economic, and Political Unrest

The social, economic, and political unrest predicted for the next decade will be unequal to that of any past century. Indeed, the imperfections of an unfettered free-market economy in the United States, as well as in Europe and Asia, could potentially lead to disruptions that dwarf the protests of the late 1960s and early 1970s, when (much like today) economic recession and an unpopular war fueled public anger and protest. The economics of hardship across all sectors of the United States coupled with the cost of the war in Iraq (estimated at $3 trillion) caused considerable dissatisfaction with the Bush administration and now generate demands on the Obama administration to end the funding of all war.

Strikes and demonstrations by workers in Europe and Asia worried about protecting their jobs and protesting the perceived threat of immigrants portend future contextual crises.

5. Public Mistrust

Public mistrust of bankers, investors, and financiers—and of what are perceived to be duplicitous heads of corporations, governments, and organizations—is rampant. It has resulted in a fierce, Darwinian competition for survival at the top.

Our largest banks, investment firms, and once-golden companies have fired CEOs, replaced corporate boards, and restructured work teams. The desperate search for those to blame, as well as for those who can save the day, have replaced efforts to repair the damage. This turmoil has led the White House to take what, at other times, would have been considered an outrageous step: the firing of the chairman and CEO of General Motors for his failure to lead a company that had been considered the bellwether of a healthy U.S. economy. In addition, the secretary of the Treasury has ordered newly appointed executives at General Motors to claim bankruptcy, against their will, and to restructure their company. The U.S. Treasury is not only monitoring and controlling the compensation levels of corporate executives, but President Obama has moved to restrict executive pay at seven of the nation's largest companies that received billions in federal aid to survive the economic crisis. In addition, he has encouraged executives to assume new responsibility for producing positive results.

6. The Growing Disparity Between Rich and Poor

The disparity between rich and poor reveals a gigantic chasm between the top executive quintile and the bottom wage-earner quintile. The gap is rapidly increasing, along with almost obscene differentials between the salaries of CEOs and those of average workers. Nearly 90 percent of stocks are now owned by 10 percent of the population, with the top 1 percent owning 51.4 percent.

Add to that increasing disparities in education and family services, and the crisis becomes even more desperate. According to the National Center for Education Statistics, only about 20 percent of Hispanic and African-American adults hold a higher-education degree as compared with about 50 percent of Caucasians. Couple that statistic with the finding that a high school diploma cuts the chances of living in poverty by half, and higher education cuts it even more. Thus, the divide will continue to widen as race, immigration status, and parents' income act as additional factors influencing the pursuit of education.

7. Inversion of Trust

The inversion of trust is rampant among those wishing to be bailed out of this crisis. In the mid-1950s, about 70 percent of Americans believed government was genuinely concerned with the common good. Trust in government began to erode in the mid-1960s and continues to decline in this new century at an accelerating rate. Recent studies indicate that only 25 percent of Americans now trust their government, and there is an apocryphal story to reinforce this perception: A government poll asked: "Do you trust the government more or less than you did five years ago?" Ten percent of those surveyed said they trusted the government more; 15 percent said they trusted it less; the remaining 75 percent refused to answer—they thought the survey was some sort of government plot to trick them!

Even those lucky enough to be employed find themselves wondering anxiously whether they will face a pink slip tomorrow. Many avoid taking risks to be leaders for fear of getting fired and thus fail to address problems or offer solutions.

8. Failure to Learn and Act

Perhaps the worst danger of all is the widespread failure to learn from the disclosures of economic greed, dishonesty, and continued blindness to lessons from the past. Paul Krugman, economist and Nobel Laureate, wrote a critique of current practices in his column in the *New York Times* from Princeton University, where he teaches. He labeled as failed the leadership of Alan Greenspan, former president of the Federal Reserve Bank, and of Robert Rubin and Larry Summers, advisors to former President Clinton and to President Obama:

> Because we're all so worried about the current crisis, it's hard to focus on the longer-term issues—on reining in the out-of-control financial system, so as to prevent or at least limit the next crisis. Yet the experience of the last decade suggests that we should be worrying about financial reform, above all regulating the "shadow banking system" at the heart of the current mess, sooner rather than later. . . . So here's my plea: Even though the incoming administration's agenda is already very full, it should not put off financial reform. The time to start preventing the next crisis is now. ("Lest We Forget," *International Herald Tribune*, November 29, 30, 2008)

We purposefully sound an alarm for leaders to act immediately and address the deep and abiding crises in our society, with the hope that they will be responsible for a future that is worth living.

Contextual Intelligence

Leaders with *contextual intelligence* seek to understand the impact of external events on their life choices and search for ethical solutions to guide others to learn to lead. They know they must master their big-picture context as well as their personal context to take leadership in their organization. They observe day-to-day interactions of staff, they question employees on every level and in every role, and they explore the requirements for success of the organizational culture. *Cultural intelligence* is a leadership skill that can be developed by anyone at any level of any organization when they perceive and understand the cultural and personal contexts that impinge on their lives.

We use the term "knowledge" as distinct from "information" or "data," because "knowledge" requires awareness, analysis, and understanding of raw information or data. Knowledge reveals profound, complex, and powerful perceptions and solutions. As a leader, you will want to seek knowledge from four primary sources:

1. *Self-knowledge* brings awareness and understanding about your values and beliefs. It forms the ground on which you stand to make ethical judgments. Self-knowledge enables you to predict the impact of your personal needs and wishes, biases, political leanings, ambitions, limitations, and strengths. It includes an awareness of your history, your role models, and your current choices and lets you see the impact of these influences on your leadership values and choices.

2. *Social-network knowledge* draws on your recognition and assessment of the information flowing around you from friends, colleagues, and acquaintances. As you process this information you arrive at the knowledge of your values and the expectations you derive from your social setting. Social-network knowledge includes an understanding of subtle signals and provides an ability to recognize themes, tendencies, and prophesies that can be so subtle they escape the notice of others.

3. *Organizational knowledge* comprises a web of themes from the culture of your workplace, school, community, volunteer site, or family. This information may be explicit, as in a publicly stated mission of your organization, or implicitly hidden in unstated cultural values, norms for behavior, and expectations for success.

4. *Stakeholder knowledge* includes the history, thoughts, expectations, needs, and desires of those who depend on your leadership. This is comprised of an understanding of the central interests of all who have a stake in the organization's success and are willing to step up to the plate to contribute to the effort. Stakeholder knowledge includes the values and needs that you must address to gain stakeholder trust.

To develop your leadership skills in mastering the external context in your life and to hone your ability to align with your internal context of values, you will need to increase your ability to perceive, judge, and deploy these four types of knowledge.

Contextual Intelligence—An Exercise

In the chart below, identify the knowledge you wish to develop as a leader and possible sources of information that you can investigate.

SELF-KNOWLEDGE   SOURCES

. . . .

. . . .

. . . .

. . . .

SOCIAL-NETWORK KNOWLEDGE   SOURCES

. . . .

. . . .

. . . .

. . . .

ORGANIZATIONAL KNOWLEDGE   SOURCES

. . . .

. . . .

. . . .

. . . .

STAKEHOLDER KNOWLEDGE   SOURCES

. . . .

. . . .

. . . .

. . . .

Leaders Take Time to Lead

The best leaders are almost obsessed with mastering the big-picture context. They do so by analyzing the history of current problems, noting trends and movements, tracking the flow of everyday events, and predicting the future. As they examine the big picture, they focus on issues in all their complexity and take account of paradoxes and the diverse implications of the problems they face before choosing a solution. Albert Einstein, that great thinker, cautioned leaders to carefully analyze problems:

> The formulation of a problem is often more essential to its solution than the solution itself, which may be merely a matter of mathematical or experimental skill. To raise new questions, new possibilities, or to regard old questions from a new angle, requires creative imagination and marks *real* advances.

Leaders learn to analyze problems and master issues by taking time and directing energy to gather information for formulating broad knowledge, even if they must venture outside their expertise. They read newspapers, review journals, study commentaries on the Web and in news media, and weigh the opinions of their favorite bloggers. They seek sources of contradictory information and are willing to entertain dissent while remaining open to paradoxical thinking that may impinge on the problem.

How many times have you said, "I didn't even have time to think?" How often have you been too busy to analyze the big picture or to collect information about the context influencing a choice you need to make? How many times have you rushed through a decision without stopping to discover what your values might be, or to strengthen your resolve, in the swirl of events that enveloped you?

Of course we were all shocked, disgusted, and saddened to learn of the torture inflicted by members of the U.S. armed forces on detainees in Abu Ghraib prison in Iraq and in other detention centers internationally. Continued revelations of the high-level Bush administration's endorsement of these tactics further dismayed the public. But the reports that seemed most deeply troubling were those reported by guards at Abu Ghraib itself or at the CIA's headquarters in Washington who knew about these practices, wanted them to cease, and yet did nothing. Their excuse was tragic: "Things were moving so fast I couldn't stop them. I didn't have the time to do anything. I didn't know what to do."

The best leaders view time as a context for their actions and know how to master it. They "slow down" time so as to better understand the problem, create powerful strategies, develop supporting alliances, marshal resources, and remain true to their values and those of the people they serve. Thus, they make wiser, stronger, more ethical decisions that conserve time, energy, and resources. Time is not their master. *Time is a context to be mastered.*

Consider the stacks of unread articles and rapid-fire e-mails waiting in a queue for your attention right now, even as you read this passage. Recall an occasion when you failed to give attention to your inner voice reminding you of the values you hold dear. Think of a time when you intended to take a stand for what you believed was right but did not stop and think about what you must do. If such examples do come to mind, notice how you failed to be a leader who mastered the context that is time.

When we coach leaders, we ask them to look through their calendars and block out time on their schedules, each day, as if they were going to attend an important meeting. This is the time they will use to focus on the big picture and listen to their inner voice. If you work in an office, you might close the door and post a "Do Not Disturb" sign outside; if you work in a cubicle, place such a sign on the edge of the enclosure. Alternatively, find an empty conference room that offers private space in which to read and think. If you are a student, find a desk in the school library or a room at home where you can concentrate on the big picture, and on any problems that bother you.

Time and Place to Consider the Context—An Exercise

This exercise is a gift to you. If you follow it, you will find your inner voice, hear what it has to tell you, and respect its message. Once you recognize yourself *in* yourself, you will never again ignore what you know is true and you will gain access to the strength and talent of your inner context.

To do the exercise, schedule an hour a day for thinking about and reviewing information so you will gain knowledge that can guide your leadership judgments. Add time for study and reflection to your already busy calendar and inform colleagues of your plan to do so, requesting that they honor your schedule. If you let them know, you will not only preserve time for yourself but also become a role model as a responsible leader who is committed to mastering the contextual framework for your work.

Activities to Consider

A. Review your priorities and identify the times you will schedule *today* to begin to master the context.

B. Add days and times to your schedule for the *rest of the week* that you will devote to mastering the context.

. . . .

. . . .

. . . .

. . . .

C. Indicate the locations in which you can meditate, read, and think things through.

· ·

· ·

· ·

· ·

D. List the changes you will make in your daily schedule that will give you time and space to master big-picture contexts for leadership decisions.

· ·

· ·

· ·

· ·

E. Note the articles you plan to read, the blogs you will visit, and the ideas you intend to explore.

· ·

· ·

· ·

· ·

F. List the people you want to encounter, the ones who have information that may be critical to your decisions or who regularly espouse ideas that run counter to your usual thinking.

G. Indicate the times when you can schedule meetings with colleagues who may have ideas that differ from yours.

. . . .

. . . .

. . . .

. . . .

H. Describe the steps you will take to meet with others and gain access to their knowledge.

. . . .

. . . .

. . . .

. . . .

I. Predict the useful insights you will have gained as a result of this process.

. . . .

. . . .

. . . .

. . . .

As you join the ranks of exemplary leaders who take responsibility for the external and internal contexts in their lives, you will overcome limiting, restrictive forces that may be distracting you. As a result, your values and inner commitments will become clearer and stronger and you will inspire trust and optimism from others, motivating them to join you in realizing your intentions for constructive change.

Where Have All the Leaders Gone?

Many of the leaders we once respected are now dead. FDR, who challenged a nation to rise above fear, is gone. Martin Luther King Jr., who taught his followers to realize the dream of equality, is gone. Albert Schweitzer, who inspired mankind with a reverence for life from the jungles of Lambaréné, is gone. Albert Einstein, who gave us a sense of unity in infinity, and of cosmic harmony, is gone. Mohandas Gandhi, John and Robert Kennedy, Anwar Sadat, Yitzak Rabin, Malcolm X—all were slain. Their lives were testimonies that we can be better than we are.

Many of today's so-called leaders, by contrast, seem to be organizational Houdinis, surrounded by sharks or shackled in a water cage, but always managing to escape with golden parachutes. Unfortunately, toxic leaders usually revert to motivating people through fear, promising what they cannot deliver, or posing as tough advocates of "reality," which they cynically misrepresent. Thus, precisely at a time when the credibility of our alleged leaders is at an all-time low, potential leaders feel most inhibited about exercising their gifts. The world is deeply troubled, searching for leaders of quality as the quantity and seriousness of our problems escalate.

Genuine leaders seem almost to be an endangered species, caught in a whirlwind of events and circumstances beyond rational control. The last two decades have witnessed a high turnover, at an appalling mortality rate—both occupational and actuarial—among true organizational leaders. The "shelf life" of college presidents and CEOs has been markedly reduced; the days of corporate chieftains who are trying to do the right thing seem to be numbered from the moment they step up to the job. Superintendents of big-city school districts last only two to three years, often citing health problems as a reason for leaving. In local communities, the burnout factor discourages neighborhood reformers from sticking to it for the long haul.

Doubtless, a number of complex factors are involved in the diminishing half-life of executive tenure: the credit crisis, hyper-competition, government bailouts, Internet volatility, turbocharged globalism, and trillion-dollar losses. In the process of writing this book, we have rounded up the usual suspects and sifted through them to discover examples of those who are heading organizations and who have discernible humane values. We have searched for leaders who can sustain themselves, maintain the pace, balance their priorities, determine what's really important, and build meaning into each day of work. Indeed, we continue to search for leaders who embrace a life of integrity, a life of the intellect, and a life of values beyond question. The stakes are high. The quality of our lives depends on the quality of our leaders. Actually, it is up to you: If you have ever had dreams of being a leader, now is the time, this is the place, and you are the one.

Leading in Spite of Circumstances

History teaches us that circumstance, happenstance, and the press of events all matter to the survival of leadership. At any moment, an accident may occur that can rob you of a chance to make a difference as a leader. Yet the following three examples tell of people who became leaders after overcoming life-threatening experiences. They remind us that our response to overwhelming disaster can give us a chance to survive a turn of fate and to realize our own destiny as leaders.

In December 1931, during a visit to New York, a middle-aged Briton was struck by a car while crossing Fifth Avenue. Badly hurt, but not so disabled that he couldn't write to the British press with his own account of the accident, the English visitor left the hospital as soon as possible with a determination to fully recuperate. Now imagine what the rise of Nazi power and World War II would have been like without the galvanizing rhetoric of this leader who was almost done in by a New York driver. The visitor was, of course, Winston Churchill.

Or imagine how different the world would be today if, in Miami in 1933, Guiseppe Zangora hadn't fatally shot Chicago Mayor Anton Cermak but instead had killed his intended victim, President-elect Franklin Delano Roosevelt. Both Churchill and Roosevelt shaped the world of their day and went on to save it. Their encounters with death came prior to their opportunities for greatness, and their stories remind us that difficult and dramatic circumstances need not block us from learning to lead.

As we reflect on the twists and turns of past leaders who danced with history, we recall the graceful steps of our colleague Barbara Nussbaum. As a spokesperson for *Ubuntu*, the indigenous leadership philosophy of South Africa, Barbara leads powerful collaborations to build an inclusive and humane community in a once-divided world. Her Jewish father, Leon, and her grandparents had fled Germany and the Nazi Holocaust to build their life in Bulawayo, Zimbabwe. Thus Leon's oldest daughter, Barbara, grew up in a small but vibrant white and Jewish community in a country where the population was 95 percent black. A serious student of ballet, with a degree in dance therapy, she was struck with rheumatoid arthritis while still a young woman. Throughout the past decade and a half her mobility improved, and she moved from Ojai, California, to Johannesburg and then to Cape Town, South Africa, to become a leading advisor to businesses, governments, and community leaders in many countries. She has also written books and articles and become a spokeswoman for the wisdom of *Ubuntu*:

> I am because you are, I became because you became; we are human beings through the eyes of other human beings; my dignity is your dignity. That is what *Ubuntu* teaches us.

If Barbara's family had not acted to save themselves, and if they had failed to seek refuge in Zimbabwe, we would have lost Barbara's leadership voice for a New South Africa.

Values Make Leaders—An Exercise

Leaders are clear about the values they hold dear and use them to deepen their identity and to make themselves known in society. Consider, for example, how

Hendrick Hertzberg assessed the contribution to leadership made by Robert F. Kennedy in his article "Scaling Mt. Kennedy: R.F.K.'s Journey from Fixer to Martyrdom" (*New Yorker*, November 20, 2000):

> Robert Kennedy, on his own, left no great legislative legacy, founded no great institution, led no great movement. His most extraordinary accomplishment— and it was extraordinary—was to embody in himself, and create in others, a kind of transcendent yearning for the possibility of redemptive change.

In the last years before his assassination, Kennedy not only strongly believed in redemptive change but demonstrated the possibility of it through his march with poor farm workers seeking a minimum wage for their back-breaking toils and his courageous act of attending rallies and demonstrations in black communities during the upheavals and near-riots that occurred on the night that Dr. King was assassinated. Throughout these later years, Kennedy spoke for those whose voices were not respected or heard.

In the exercise below, we ask you to write a paragraph that describes your own leadership legacy, the one you hope to leave by living your values, by taking a stand for what is important to you, and by demonstrating what your life is about. After you have articulated the gift you want to leave for future generations, indicate at least one action you have taken, one noticeable result you have achieved, one piece of evidence that demonstrates the values most important to you.

Questions to Consider

A. What is the one value for which you wish to be remembered in your family, your community, your work, in your life?

B. List actions you have taken that demonstrate this value or outcomes you have achieved as a result of holding this value.

. . . .

. . . .

. . . .

. . . .

Leaders Live Their Values

When leaders are clear about their values and live them, even the smallest gestures can have a huge impact. Consider Nelson Mandela, for instance. When he was elected president of South Africa in 1995, he had the strongly held value of building a united country in which there was lasting peace between whites and blacks. Previously, under apartheid, the game of rugby had been segregated and, as a national sport, it had become a symbol to blacks of their oppression. Black people had been barred from playing on national teams, from attending national games, even from identifying with the sport.

During games involving the national team, known as the Springboks, many blacks took delight in rooting for the opposing team that represented another country. Yet, when the Springboks met New Zealand in the finals for the World Cup in 1995, the new president attended the game sporting a Springboks hat and jersey! As soon as he entered the stadium in his uniform, cries of "Nelson, Nelson" burst from many white fans in the bleachers. After South Africa won the game, President Mandela came down from the stands to the field to congratulate the captain, François Pienaar. Mandela reportedly said: "François, thank you very much for what you have done for our country."

Pienaar, a white man who had accepted apartheid, and endorsed it, replied: "No, Mr. President. Thank you for what you have done for our country." When the two men hugged, a powerful symbol communicated Mandela's value of a racially unified society. Mandela's simple act, of wearing that jersey and hat, remains a vivid reminder that a single person can change millions of lives and reshape the world by standing up for his or her values.

Leadership is indeed a matter of values, and thus we must ask: "Leadership for what purpose?" If we consider a diverse group of leaders—Sitting Bull, Cesar Chavez, Susan B. Anthony, and Kofi Annan—and ask what they have in common, we realize they stood for values that guided their actions so powerfully that followers were willing to stand with them.

We may never develop an all-encompassing theory of leadership. However, based on the breakthroughs in leadership studies that originated in the mid-twentieth century during that fertile period for the social sciences just after World War II, we can make an evolutionary leap if we consider the way a new way of thinking emerged in those years.

After the giants—Roosevelt, Churchill, and Stalin—made their marks as solitary charismatic leaders, the emphasis on leadership shifted to a study of followers, groups, and systems. A new analysis was forged in response to the Holocaust, and a determination was made to prevent future such horrors. One leading thinker who suggested new definitions of leadership was the great Kurt Lewin, a refugee from Hitler's Germany who was grateful almost to the point of giddiness to be in the United States. Lewin was a brilliant teacher who urged the best minds in his generation to address the most urgent social problems and apply the tools of psychology to understand and explain such terrible conundrums as the rise of fascism, racial injustice, and other societal crises. His new *zeitgeist* was informed by a hunger to understand why the world had gone mad. He was committed to contributing to those who had not perished at the hands of fascism, and to join with other scholars who were empowered by new tools such as systems theory and had a willingness to collaborate across disciplinary boundaries.

The theory of leadership inherited from Lewin was further developed by his contemporaries and disciples: Douglas McGregor, Peter Drucker, Harold Levin, Jean Lipman-Blumen, Abraham Maslow, Theodor Adorno, Rosabeth Moss Kantor, and Joan Goldsmith and Warren Bennis. They were part of an interdisciplinary intellectual movement that built a democratic theory of leadership, supported by cognitive scientists, social psychologists, sociologists, neuroscientists, anthropologists, biologists, ethicists, political scientists, historians, sociobiologists, and others. As a result, the study of leadership became increasingly collaborative, with many fine minds from many powerful disciplines working together.

These breakthroughs in thinking about humankind have inspired the two of us to turn our attention from the mastery of context to the leadership competency that is founded on self-knowledge. No leader who knows him- or herself can possibly commit atrocities against another human being. You will see that this is true once you have perceived the context of your life and the values you cherish. To assist you in developing as a self-aware, humane leader, the next chapter provides an opportunity for you to explore your capacity for self-knowledge and to consider the critical part it plays in your development as a leader.

4 Knowing Yourself: Competency Two

*If God, for a second, forgot what I have become and granted me a little bit more
of life, I would use it to the best of my ability. . . .*

*I have learned so much with you all, I have learned that everybody wants to
live on top of the mountain, without knowing that true happiness is obtained in
the journey taken and the form used to reach the top of the hill. . . .*

*Tomorrow is never guaranteed to anyone, young or old. Today could be the last
time to see your loved ones, which is why you mustn't wait; do it today, in case
tomorrow never arrives. I am sure you will be sorry you wasted the opportunity
today to give a smile, a hug, a kiss, and that you were too busy to grant them
their last wish. . . . Nobody will know you for your secret thoughts. Ask the Lord
for wisdom and strength to express them. . . .*

> **—Gabriel García Márquez**
> **E-mail message, August 2008**

THE MUCH-ACCLAIMED COLUMBIAN NOVELIST AND NOBEL LAUREATE
Gabriel García Márquez wrote this intimate message to friends when he
became ill with cancer. His words remind us that each day, each moment provides an opportunity to become who we are as a person as well as a leader. We
join Márquez in urging that you not waste a minute in learning to know yourself.

Leaders have positive self-regard and recognize their ability to contribute to
the quality of life of those around them. As you learn to know yourself, you will

be open to new experiences, seek new and different sources of information, observe yourself with a critical eye, and hear your inner voice as a leader.

Searching for self-knowledge is a bit like climbing a mountain. Both can be sources of immense happiness. The joy of finally seeing yourself clearly can be as fulfilling as reaching the top of the peak. Insights will come instantly, like lightning bolts striking on a hike, or will slowly emerge like the mountains in passing scenery. On your journey, you will discover multifaceted aspects of yourself and reach a moment when your inner voice rings with knowledge about who you are. Then you will truly understand how to express your leadership talents. This is the goal of mastering the second competency, the one of knowing yourself.

Leaders develop self-knowledge by exploring ideas, by discovering ways of being, by perceiving the larger context of their lives, and by listening to the inner messages from their hearts. They are willing to risk reevaluating what they hold as true, even their most treasured beliefs, and they often challenge their own assumptions. They rapidly readjust their visions, and their goals and priorities, when fresh insights reveal that they are headed in the wrong direction.

In the process of learning about themselves, leaders continually align actions with intentions. They evaluate themselves to make sure that what they do results in a moral and ethical life. They seek to maintain and deepen their integrity and to experience themselves as whole and integrated human beings. When they achieve this enlightened state, they engage others to join in a shared purpose.

Shifting the Leadership Paradigm

The failures of leadership on the world stage call for reevaluating the prevailing paradigms of leadership. The concept of "paradigm" implies the framework and contextual perspective through which we view our world. A shift away from widely held paradigms of leadership that we advocate has far-reaching consequences for individuals as well as for society as a whole.

For example, the scientific knowledge resulting from Galileo's discovery that our planet circles the sun not only transformed fifteenth-century Europe's thinking about the earth's placement in the universe but also led to changed views about the role of the father as the center of family life and the king as the sole leader of the state. At that turning point, personal, social, and political thought accepted more complex, nuanced beliefs about multiple sources of power, authority, and knowledge.

Current significant shifts in social paradigms include increased acceptance of leadership by women in government, religious organizations, and business; the perception of Russia as an ally of the United States; and the belief that *all* Americans are entitled to civil rights, legal marriage, and voting privileges regardless of race, ethnicity, and sexual orientation.

In our view, another new paradigm is needed—one that provides a context for leaders to understand their responsibility to lead the transformation of economic, social, and political conditions. This new paradigm of leadership must be based on ethical values and a commitment to be fully integrated and evolved human beings.

Mastering a New Paradigm—An Exercise

With the emergence of a new leadership paradigm, aspects of the old way of thinking intrude from time to time. Three elements of that outdated paradigm are particularly pernicious and dysfunctional. This exercise will enable you to heighten your awareness of the old paradigm and create alternative ways of thinking about the leadership you value. When you consider each element of the outdated paradigm, observe the extent to which you have believed in it, and indicate how this belief may have caused you to hesitate and be uncertain about becoming a strong and effective leader.

1. Leaders Are Great Men Who Are More Qualified to Lead and Solve Problems Than I Can Ever Be

According to the *silver-spoon* theory of leadership, leaders are born with a correct lineage and endowed with physical beauty, winning personalities, and wealth and power. As a result, they have an innate overriding authority that qualifies them to lead. In this paradigm, followers lack any choice in the matter and are resigned to apathy, cynicism, and mindless obedience.

Your Alternative Paradigm:

. . . .

. . . .

. . . .

. . . .

. . . .

. . . .

. . . .

2. Good Management Makes Successful Organizations

In this nineteenth-century managerial model of organizations, efficient top-down managers who exercised command and control to get the job done were expected to provide short-term results and successfully impact the bottom line. Today, the same paradigm results in hierarchical, bureaucratic, and autocratic forms of management that prevent true leaders from emerging.

Your Alternative Paradigm:

. . . .

. . . .

. . . .

. . . .

. . . .

. . . .

. . . .

3. Mistakes Are to Be Avoided at All Costs

In this paradigm, leaders never fail and never make obvious mistakes; failures are hidden, swept under the rug, denied, and dealt with by blaming others; and organizational behavior is characterized by risk aversion and fear of discovery.

Your Alternative Paradigm:

. . . .

. . . .

. . . .

. . . .

. . . .

. . . .

. . . .

As you learn to lead, you have an opportunity to create a new paradigm to guide your thinking. It will encourage you to "do the right thing" rather than simply focusing on "doing things right." Indeed, this new view of leadership will support you in taking risks and learning from the failures you encounter along the way.

To initiate a new paradigm in your life, you must think in new ways: Leaders learn from their mistakes, adapt to changing conditions, and know that not everything can be predicted in advance of taking action. They also take prompts from their internal compasses and take risks. Even if they stumble in the process, they invent outlandish ideas, learn from those of lower rank, and adapt to the constant demands of change. Indeed, accidents, chaos, and indeterminacy are inevitable when leaders innovate, and motivate followers by their courage.

Failures Offer Opportunities

Among the defining qualities of leaders are their adaptive capacity, their resilience, and their acceptance of failure as a natural part of life. True leaders embrace mistakes and think of them as "trials and errors," "glitches," "hashes," "miscues," "false starts," "wrong turns," or "curves in the road." They do not view failure as terminal and lifeless. They actually *look forward* to identifying mistakes, believing that if they do not make them they are not taking enough risks to find the *best* solution, or not giving it their all, or not being courageous enough to take the blame when things go wrong. They do not want to miss any opportunity to learn or to change for the better.

In the midst of the recent financial crisis, pundits and politicians have debated the origins of many problems. They have ascribed blame to others, refused to own their own complicity, and avoided putting their considerable intelligence to work in finding solutions. In Washington, D.C., as well as on Wall Street and Main Street, economists and political personalities searched for culprits. The candidates for blame included Democrats, Republicans, the Federal Reserve Bank, an overzealous home-lending industry, traders in derivatives, major lending and commercial banks, President Bush and his administration, and President Clinton along with his advisors, who advocated for deregulation. All of them have been accused of causing the "meltdown." It was only when President Obama took office and declared "I am to blame, the buck stops here, I must fix it" that we had a leader who was willing to put an end to the wasted energy of the dance-of-blame and redirect his cabinet to devise creative and hard-wrought solutions. True leaders take responsibility for failures and openly and actively acknowledge their mistakes. They put themselves in a unique position to discover solutions that have never before been conceived of or considered by others.

How many pensions and retirement accounts would have been saved if managers of failing banks and government regulators had revealed and addressed the investment errors in the runaway grab for sub-prime mortgage profits and confronted fraud in their own organizations? While it may not be easy to admit making an error or to search for the cause of one's own mistake, doing so can be a liberating experience for oneself and can increase the possibility of preventing a repeated disaster for everyone else.

Karl Wallenda, the great aerialist whose life was endangered every time he crossed the tightrope, risked all—as do many leaders who seem to be operating on solid ground. For most of his life, he had carefully and devotedly focused on the task of overcoming the risks that were inevitable in his work. Wallenda was passionate about his art, often remarking that "being on the tightrope is living; everything else is waiting." Unfortunately his life's work was abruptly halted when he fell to his death in 1978 while traversing a high wire seventy-five feet long that had been stretched between two towering office buildings in downtown San Juan, Puerto Rico.

Soon after he died, his wife, also an aerialist, reflected on that fateful walk. She described it as "perhaps his most dangerous," and then added:

> All Karl thought about for three straight months prior to that walk was not falling. It was the first time he'd ever thought about that, and it seemed to me that he put his energies into not falling rather than walking the tightrope.

In fact, his fall was caused by that fear. As he began to fall, he grasped his balance stick for too long a time and, instead of tossing it aside so he could grip the high wire and break his fall, he froze in fear and did not respond to save himself. It was precisely when this master aerialist poured his energies into *not falling* that he became virtually destined to fall to his death.

The same is true of all leaders: If they lose their focus on reaching their goals, and instead they obsess about *not failing*, they will inevitably fail.

For many of us the word "failure" carries a sense of finality, representing a dead thing and hopeless discouragement. But for most successful leaders, failure can be a chance for a new beginning, a springboard of hope. Ray Meyer, one of the winningest coaches in college basketball, viewed failure in this positive way. His team won twenty-nine straight home-court victories, and then lost a game. His response was: "Great! Now we can start concentrating on winning, *not on not losing*." Meyer wanted the team members to have positive goals; he wanted them to avoid looking backward, dredging up excuses, or blaming each other for mistakes.

Failure: Springboard of Hope—An Exercise

Where did we first learn how to view mistakes and failure? A young child, beginning to walk, can teach us about failure. Children fall hundreds of times before they get the knack of standing on two feet and propelling themselves forward. They do not stop to worry about mistakes or feel guilty or embarrassed by their attempts to master this simple but necessary skill.

Do you remember when you first learned to ride a bicycle? When you fell off you probably didn't give up biking forever with deep remorse about falling. Rather, you got back on your bike even though you may have skinned your knee, and you continued to weave and wobble until you mastered bike riding for a lifetime.

In the following guided imagery exercise, we provide an opportunity for you to identify any core experiences that have helped shape your attitudes and feeling about your own failures. Through this guided exploration to view your internal images you can understand more clearly the origins of your views.

We suggest that you invite a spouse, partner, or colleague to assist you by reading the instructions to you—and, later, you can switch roles, giving your partner a chance at the exercise. Alternatively, if you are in a team, one person can read the instructions aloud and have an opportunity at another time to experience the process.

Before you close your eyes and begin the guided imagery process, review the instructions and let feelings, thoughts, and images enter your consciousness. Feelings and emotions may arise, and when they do, let them come so that you fully recognize and experience them. Thoughts and insights may emerge, and when they do, notice them and return to the exercise without letting them distract you. Images and memories from the past may appear, and if they do, welcome them. There are no mistakes in this exercise. Anything you feel, understand, or see is fine, as it will provide information to you about yourself.

Your only tasks are to follow the instructions read by your partner or team member and to accept whatever comes to you. If you are with a group, do not open your eyes to observe what is happening with others or interrupt the exercise for any reason. Below are a number of phrases, suggested pauses, and acknowledgments for the reader to use so that the process will unfold smoothly and effectively.

Steps in Guided Imagery Process

Sit in a comfortable position with your back against a chair and your feet placed firmly on the floor. [Pause.] Good.

Uncross your legs and rest your hands in a relaxed, open position on your lap. [Pause.] Good.

Gently let your eyelids get heavy and your eyes slowly close. Inhale deep breaths and slowly release them. [Pause.] With each breath, let your eyes relax and let your body release any tension. [Pause.] Good.

Notice any sounds or movements in the room and take your attention from these sounds and movements. [Pause.] Good.

Let any thoughts come into your consciousness, and release these thoughts. [Pause.] Good.

Let any emotions come into your consciousness, and release these emotions. [Pause.] Good.

Let any memories or images from the past come into your consciousness, and release these memories and images. [Pause.] Good.

Now you are sitting comfortably in your chair. [Pause.] You have let go of any noise or movement in the room. [Pause.] You have released all your tensions, thoughts, emotions, and images from your past so your mind is empty. [Pause.] Good.

Focus your attention on each of your feet and each of your legs. If you notice any tension, release it. [Pause.] Good.

Focus your attention on your abdomen and lower body. If you notice any tension, release it. [Pause.] Good.

Focus your attention on your chest, shoulders, and arms. If you notice any tension, release it. [Pause.] Good.

Focus your attention on your neck, head, and face. If you notice any tension, release it. [Pause.] Good.

Now you are fully relaxed and you are open and available to whatever comes to you. [Pause.] Good.

Remember a time when you failed at something. [Pause.] Just let the memory come into your consciousness. Stay with the memory for a moment or two. [Slightly longer pause.] Notice what you are doing. [Pause.] How old are you? What are you wearing? What are you saying? [Pause.] What are you feeling? Who is there with you? [Pause.] Notice how you felt in that time. [Pause.]

Remember a time when someone you were close to was told that he or she was a failure. [Pause.] Just let the memory come into your consciousness. [Pause.] Who told this person that he or she was a failure? How did you feel when you heard this label applied to another person? What decisions did you make as a result? [Pause.]

Stay with the memory for a minute or two. [Pause.] Notice what this person did that others thought was a failure. [Pause.] Notice how this person felt. [Pause.] Notice how you felt. [Pause.] Good.

Remember a time when someone told you, directly or indirectly, that *you* were a failure. [Pause.] Just let the memory come into your consciousness. Stay with the memory for a minute or two. [Slightly longer pause.] Notice who it was that told you that you were a failure. [Pause.] Notice how you felt. [Pause.] Good.

Remember a time when you were a success, or someone told you, directly or indirectly, that you succeeded. [Pause.] Just let this memory come into your consciousness. Stay with the memory for a minute or two. [Pause.] What were you doing at that time? How old were you? How did you feel when you were doing it? Who was with you? Who told you that you were a success? [Pause.] Notice how you felt. [Pause.] Good.

Let any feelings you have associated with these incidents emerge and let them go. [Pause.] Good.

Notice if you have anything to say to the person who told you that you were a failure, and say it to this person in your mind now. [Pause.] Good.

Notice if you have anything to say to the person who told you that you were a success, and say it to this person in your mind now. [Pause.] Good.

If you have feelings about any failure and you want to say goodbye to that experience, say goodbye now. [Pause.] Good.

Now let go of all the images you have in your mind, and just relax. [Pause.] Good.

In a relaxed state, let any feelings, thoughts, or pictures come to the surface and release them. [Pause.]

Keep your eyes closed as you bring your consciousness back into the room. After I count to five, you can open your eyes.

As you wait for the count of five, feel the back of the chair supporting your
body and the floor supporting your feet. [Pause.] Good.

Notice the noises in the room and the movements around you. [Pause.] Good.

As I count to five, return your attention to the room. One. [Pause.] Two.
[Pause.] Three. [Pause.] Four. [Pause.] Five. [Pause.] Open your eyes, and say
hello to someone in the room. Thank you.

When you complete this process, turn to a partner and share any insights,
feelings, body sensations, and images that appeared to you. Let the other person
know anything you have learned about failure; then ask that person to describe
his or her experience to you.

To shift your thinking about failure, consider this wonderful story told by the
Pulitzer Prize–winning playwright David Hare. He described a time early in his
career when he was taught an important lesson about failure by Joseph Papp, the
famed impresario and theater director, who had taken a risk to present one of
Hare's early plays at the Public Theater in New York. Hare shared his experience
at a memorial for Papp in November 1991:

> The greatest thing Joe ever did was when we did *The Knife*. There was a party
> afterward and the reviews were read. The *Times* review was absolutely dis-
> mal. He read it out line-by-line and the whole room went completely silent. It
> meant that we had lost over a million dollars. At the end he said, "That is not
> what I call a good review." Then he turned to me and said, "What do you want
> to do in my theater next?"

When Papp confronted the dismal review directly and in detail, he demonstrated his belief in Hare's work and signaled that Hare might learn from the
criticism of his play, and improve it to write a success. In fact he did, and created many hit plays that were produced and directed in Joe Papp's theater!

Shifting Our Paradigm—An Exercise

The questions in this exercise ask you to consider how your family members have regarded failure, both in general and in relation to you. After you respond to the questions below, you may want to discuss your insights with family members and/or childhood friends to compare your memories with the ones they have about you.

Questions to Consider

A. What messages did members of your family give to you about failure? How were these messages communicated, and how did you react to them?

. . . .

. . . .

. . . .

. . . .

. . . .

. . . .

. . . .

B. How were you treated when you failed? Which family members let you know you had failed, and how did they communicate their views? How did you respond to their messages?

. . . .

. . . .

. . . .

. . . .

. . . .

. . . .

. . . .

C. Regarding the person who most strongly influenced your view of yourself and your failures, what motivated him or her to send those messages to you?

. . . .

. . . .

. . . .

. . . .

. . . .

. . . .

. . . .

D. What decisions did you make about failure as a result of these experiences?

. . . .

. . . .

. . . .

. . . .

. . . .

. . . .

. . . .

E. How have your past experiences influenced your current messages about failure that you send to others in your home and at work, and to yourself?

. . . .

. . . .

. . . .

. . . .

. . . .

. . . .

. . . .

F. In what ways have you communicated your views about failure to those you love and to colleagues whom you coach and mentor?

. . . .

. . . .

. . . .

. . . .

. . . .

. . . .

. . . .

G. What impact have your views had on your relationships with loved ones, colleagues, superiors, and subordinates?

. . . .

. . . .

. . . .

. . . .

. . . .

. . . .

. . . .

It may be difficult to face any dysfunctional influences you may have received from your family members who love you and whom you love, but when you trace the roots of your beliefs about failure and you take responsibility for their origins, you will welcome your insights because they will free you to transform yourself as a leader and to develop different attitudes toward mistakes and failures.

Learning to Lead Through Crucible Experiences

Learning, creativity, participation, innovation, flexibility, and effective communication are by-products of a leader's openness to mistakes, problems, and failures. Admitting failure allows you to learn more about yourself and about the contexts in which you make choices. Many of the leaders we have cited—Mandela, Churchill, Eleanor and Franklin Roosevelt, Gore, and Obama—have shown that they not only recognized their contributions to their failures but thrived on learning from these mistakes, and, in doing so, naturally inspired confidence, loyalty, and commitment in others by the ways they dealt with adversity. Indeed, one of the most reliable indicators and predictors of effective leadership is an individual's ability to find meaning in negative events, to learn even from the most trying circumstances, and to inspire others with their tenacious hold on life and learning. Put another way, conquering adversity—and emerging stronger than ever—makes for extraordinary leaders.

Difficult and, in some cases, life-threatening events are what we call "crucibles." Such events involve severe tests of patience or belief, or difficult trials, and they are characterized by a confluence of threatening intellectual, social, economic, or political forces. Leaders often find that in these crucibles they forge a new identity when they find in themselves the wherewithal to overcome their crises and come through them transformed into more capable leaders.

One example of such a leader is our dear friend Sidney Rittenberg, the author of *The Man Who Stayed Behind*. Sidney, a U.S. citizen, spent sixteen years in Chinese prisons, much of these in solitary confinement, and when he emerged in 1980, he was determinedly committed to building bridges between China and his own country and to bring democracy to the people of China. Sidney's resilience, reinforced and strengthened in the crucible of prison, is the single most important quality in his leadership. Now in his eighties, Sidney lives an active, productive, influential, and peaceful life with his wife Yulin and their four children and three grandchildren. He is not embittered by his past. Rather, he is clear about his calling, and able to teach young leaders and assist organizations in the United States to work with Chinese partners to build better lives for all people.

Not everyone faces as dramatic a crucible as Sidney's, and not everyone who is severely tested is able to extract strength and wisdom from the most trying circumstances. Yet, much as alchemists used crucibles in the hopes of turning other elements into gold, great leaders emerge in their own lives as a result of how they deal with their crucibles.

Reflecting on Life's Crucibles—An Exercise

It may be difficult or painful to reflect on any crucibles you may have encountered in your life. If you are able to do so, you may gain insights to enable you to become a more effective leader. After you have completed the questions below, share your responses with a trusted colleague or family member and benefit from his or her feedback.

Questions to Consider

A. What were the most difficult or threatening experiences you encountered in your life? If you had any crucibles, how did you change as a result of facing them and overcoming them?

. . . .

. . . .

. . . .

. . . .

. . . .

. . . .

. . . .

B. In what ways might you use the leadership strengths and talents you developed when you faced your crucibles in the past to more effectively deal with today's challenges?

. . . .

. . . .

. . . .

. . . .

. . . .

. . . .

. . . .

C. What scars from past experiences remain for you to heal from so that you can become a more effective leader?

. . . .

. . . .

. . . .

. . . .

. . . .

. . . .

. . . .

If you face further crucibles in the future, you can continue to develop as a leader by asking yourself: "What can I draw from my strengths and knowledge to sustain myself and overcome these difficulties?" Your answers to this question will contribute to your power in being a leader.

Personal Values Inspire Effective Leaders

In Chapter 3 we introduced an important leadership competency, that of "mastering the context." This competency includes understanding the external context, which comprises the world in which you live, as well as the internal context, which includes your *values* and the *principles* that guide your thoughts and actions.

There are five key values that, when embraced and lived, enable leaders to achieve outstanding accomplishments. As you consider the values below, you will become clearer about those you cherish and what to include in your goals for the future. After you have reviewed all five values and identified your goals for expressing or strengthening them, consider whether there are any values we have not included that you want to add to the list.

Defining Leadership Values—An Exercise

1. Clear Communication

Leaders clearly communicate their goals, performance expectations, and feedback to others. The best leaders place a high value on open, honest, and direct communication. They support both individual and team achievements and insist on value-based guidelines that they jointly create for better work results and career advancement.

Circle a number that indicates how strongly you hold this value:

Strong Value   1   2   3   4   5   **Weak Value**

Questions to Consider

A. What are my goals for communicating more clearly and effectively?

. . . .

. . . .

. . . .

. . . .

. . . .

. . . .

. . . .

B. How can I powerfully express my goals for my own work and communicate them to others to gain their support?

. . . .

. . . .

. . . .

. . . .

. . . .

. . . .

. . . .

C. How can I communicate more clearly my expectations for the work of others? How can I share these expectations so they will be effectively received by others and contribute to successful results?

. . . .

. . . .

. . . .

. . . .

. . . .

. . . .

. . . .

2. Ethical Practices

Leaders are committed to living their ethics and values. They reward the ethical and value-based behaviors of their colleagues and teach their values by modeling what they believe as well as by coaching and mentoring others.

Circle a number that indicates how strongly you hold this value:

Strong Value   **1**   **2**   **3**   **4**   **5**   **Weak Value**

Questions to Consider

A. What are the ethical principles that I value?

. . . .

. . . .

. . . .

. . . .

. . . .

. . . .

. . . .

B. How well do I live by these principles? What can I do to improve? How can I support others in living more ethically?

. . . .

. . . .

. . . .

. . . .

. . . .

. . . .

. . . .

C. What ethics are openly and explicitly valued by my organization? How can I more effectively build ethics into what we do and how we do it?

. . . .

. . . .

. . . .

. . . .

. . . .

. . . .

. . . .

D. How can I better support ethical behavior among my colleagues, team members, and others in my organization? Are there significant differences between my ethics and those of my colleagues? How can I bridge this gap?

. . . .

. . . .

. . . .

. . . .

. . . .

. . . .

. . . .

3. Diversity

Leadership thrives in a workforce that is diverse in race, gender, ethnicity, sexual orientation, age, handicaps, thinking styles, past experiences, creative ideas, and perspectives. The best leaders are those who learn from the rich backgrounds, ideas, contributions, and abilities of a diverse workforce and are actively engaged in increasing diversity, especially among those in positions of influence and power.

Circle a number that indicates how strongly you hold this value:

Strong Value   1   2   3   4   5   **Weak Value**

Questions to Consider

A. How can I increase my capacity to understand and support others who are different from me?

. . . .

. . . .

. . . .

. . . .

. . . .

. . . .

. . . .

B. How can I encourage greater diversity in positions of influence and power in my organization?

. . . .

. . . .

. . . .

. . . .

. . . .

. . . .

. . . .

C. How can I reward diverse styles, values, and points of view in my organization, community, and family?

. . . .

. . . .

. . . .

. . . .

. . . .

. . . .

. . . .

D. How can I include the diversity of backgrounds and talents of those around me to achieve my goals?

. . . .

. . . .

. . . .

. . . .

. . . .

. . . .

. . . .

4. Ongoing Recognition and Support

Leaders provide ongoing recognition and empowerment for teams and individuals who contribute to the success of joint endeavors. In addition, they acknowledge their own mistakes, recognize the contributions of others, and assist colleagues in solving problems by offering a broad range of ideas, resources, and motivating encouragements.

Circle a number that indicates how strongly you hold this value:

Strong Value   1   2   3   4   5   **Weak Value**

Questions to Consider

A. How can I recognize the achievements of others more openly and more often?

. . . .

. . . .

. . . .

. . . .

. . . .

. . . .

. . . .

B. How can I further encourage others with support that goes beyond what I am already doing for them?

. . . .

. . . .

. . . .

. . . .

. . . .

. . . .

. . . .

C. How can I create rich, varied and equitable systems of rewards and recognition for my team/organization?

. . . .

. . . .

. . . .

. . . .

. . . .

. . . .

. . . .

D. How can I do more to support not just those who agree with my ideas but also those who are critical of them?

. . . .

. . . .

. . . .

. . . .

. . . .

. . . .

. . . .

5. Participatory Empowerment

Leaders encourage participation in decision-making, and they share power, authority, and responsibility for outcomes. They do so to improve results, increase satisfaction, and empower others to be successful.

Circle a number that indicates how strongly you hold this value:

Strong Value   **1**   **2**   **3**   **4**   **5**   **Weak Value**

Questions to Consider

A. How can I encourage greater participation in decision-making by my family, by team members, and by those in my community?

. . . .

. . . .

. . . .

. . . .

. . . .

. . . .

. . . .

B. What can I do to empower and include others with whom I work?

. . . .

. . . .

. . . .

. . . .

. . . .

. . . .

. . . .

C. How can I increasingly transfer authority and responsibility to others?

. . . .

. . . .

. . . .

. . . .

. . . .

. . . .

. . . .

D. What can I do to enable colleagues to empower one another and achieve greater satisfaction when we succeed?

. . . .

. . . .

. . . .

. . . .

. . . .

. . . .

. . . .

6. Additional Values

Leaders have their own unique set of values that may not be apparent to others. If this is true for you, in that you have values we have not mentioned and are important to you, please write about them.

. . . .

. . . .

. . . .

. . . .

. . . .

. . . .

. . . .

Questions to Consider

A. What goals do I want to achieve in order to fully implement my values?

. . . .

. . . .

. . . .

. . . .

. . . .

. . . .

. . . .

B. How can I express my values so others can support me in achieving my goals?

. . . .

. . . .

. . . .

. . . .

. . . .

. . . .

. . . .

C. How will I know I've achieved my goals, and how will I acknowledge my achievements?

. . . .

. . . .

. . . .

. . . .

. . . .

. . . .

. . . .

In the next chapter we ask you to find your vision for the future—a vision that will express your values and support your goals and inspire others to join you in achieving them. Mastering your ability to create powerful visions will not only enhance your success in realizing your dreams, you will deepen your knowledge of yourself as a leader. Once you discover your vision for your work, your life, and your world, you will welcome yourself with appreciation, delight, and a new found love for who you truly are.

5 Creating a Powerful Vision: Competency Three

It was December 22, 1998. It wasn't just any holiday party. My partner Eileen and I were at the White House. We stood in the East Room, and drank it all in. It left us dizzy to consider the people who had stood where we were standing. There was music and people were dancing. I turned to Eileen and asked her to dance. She turned back to me with the look I've seen thousands of times—the "are you nuts?" look. We stood quietly and then I tried again. "It's our house too, you know." We didn't dance well and we didn't dance for long but in that moment, both literally and figuratively, the White House was ours.

> —Joan Garry
> E-mail message, August 2008

LEADERS COME IN EVERY SIZE, SHAPE, COLOR, AND ORIENTATION, and they share at least one trait. They all have a passion for a guiding purpose, a dedication to an overarching vision. Leaders are more than goal-directed, they are *vision*-directed, and they drive these visions to realize powerful results.

Leaders are the most results-oriented individuals in the world. Joan Garry, a longtime leader in the struggle to win human and legal rights for gays and lesbians, has the gift of translating her dreams into inspiring visions that encourage all who encounter them to join her in the efforts she so passionately advocates. Her vision for the White House was that this symbol of democracy belongs to everyone and is large enough to include all of us: "rich, poor, black, brown, white, gay, straight, young, old, men, women."

Leaders get results with their compelling visions, their intensity, and their determination. When they are explicit about what they believe and what they intend to do, people are drawn to them in a magnetic dynamic. Visionary leaders are so intent on what they are doing, they are almost like children, completely absorbed in building a castle in a sandbox, and attracting everyone around them to join in.

Passionately Committing to a Vision

Visions communicate a leader's intentions with a passion that grabs others and gets them on the bandwagon to lend their support.

Sergio Comissioná, the renowned conductor of the Houston Symphony Orchestra, was a leader in the world of music. When musicians who worked with him were asked what Comissioná was like, they answered, "Terrific. He does not waste our time." Comissioná transmitted his vision with unbridled clarity to his players about what he wanted from them. He knew precisely and emphatically what he expected to hear at any given moment. His undeviating attention to outcomes had the intended effect because others knew what he wanted and what he envisioned; as one member of Comissioná's orchestra poetically put it, they understood "the maestro's tapestry of intentions."

The leaders we *want* to follow have not just passion but also the ability to express it, as did Comissioná—a brilliant conductor of gorgeous music that transported the listener to new realms.

The passionate visions of many leaders are glimmers of possibility in the mind's eye of the leader, different from missions or goals because they are less concrete—yet they have substance, form, and color. Such visions are direct portals that connect the world to our psyches. They are links to reality and shape our dreams into clear images.

Visions are often accompanied by passion, and the passion of leaders is often intense. The leaders who communicate their passion give hope and inspiration to others, and those who live their visions passionately, with enthusiasm and vitality, demonstrate an unswerving commitment to achieving their dreams. T. E. Lawrence, the almost mythic leader known as "Lawrence of Arabia," observed:

> All men dream: but not equally. Those who dream by night in the dusty recesses of their minds awake to find that it was vanity: but the dreamers of the day are dangerous men, for they may act their dreams with open eyes, to make it possible.

Although Lawrence's vision carried him and his followers to a bloody end, we can learn from him that if leaders intend to make changes in their world and their lives, they must transform their visions from dreamlike fantasies into results in the harsh realities of daylight.

Your vision begins with dreams. They reveal an image of a future to which to commit. From dreams, you can articulate your vision and include your highest ethics and most cherished values. This vision will empower you to produce extraordinary results, inspire you to do your job, and enable you to motivate others to join you in turning your ideas into actions. Here are the key qualities of a leader's vision. Consider them as a guide that can inspire you to find your own.

- A vision engages your heart and your spirit.
- A vision taps into embedded concerns and needs.
- A vision is something worth going for.

- A vision is by definition a little cloudy and grand (if it were clear, it wouldn't be a vision).
- A vision is simple.
- A vision is a living document that can always be updated and expanded.
- A vision provides a starting place from which to get to greater and greater levels of specificity.
- A vision asserts what you and your colleagues want to create.
- A vision provides meaning to the work done by you and your colleagues.
- A vision is based in two deep human needs: attaining the highest quality and expressing the most passionate dedication.

In your heart of hearts, there is a dream for the future that you may not have recognized, acknowledged, or made explicit in your consciousness. This dream may have guided you in the past, but it may have been dormant and unconscious. It may be driving your current endeavors, and you may not have recognized its power. As you develop your leadership skills, your challenge will be to find that hidden dream, turn it into a vision, articulate it with care and style, and commit with passion to achieving it.

Creating a Passionate Vision for the World—An Exercise

In the following exercise, we ask you to open your eyes and become a "dreamer of the day." When you dream, whether you do so freely, openly, vigorously or audaciously, you become dangerous, with a passion to make your vision come true. We challenge you to become dangerous and create a vision to light up your life.

As you begin creating a vision for the big picture and thinking about your society, your community, your workplace, your school, or your family, you must consider the context influencing your choices, your identity, and your role as a leader. Your vision of the future will not only transform your thinking, it will allow you to trust yourself. Let your vision reveal the hidden hopes that you may have stuck in the corners of your mind and the secret wishes that lie at the center of your heart.

Steps to Consider

A. Picture yourself in the future, and envision a time and location that are pleasing to you. Actually see yourself in that future. What kind of society or world would you like to create?

. . . .

. . . .

. . . .

. . . .

. . . .

. . . .

. . . .

B. Express your passion for this vision. Choose any medium that allows you to give form and shape to your passion. You may want to write a poem, sketch a picture, or paint a painting; you may want to record a piece of music or write the words to a song; you may want to choreograph a dance or act out your passion in a skit. Write down why you feel passionately about your vision, and describe how you'd like to express it.

. . . .

. . . .

. . . .

. . . .

. . . .

. . . .

. . . .

C. Listen to your inner voice and feel the emotions in your heart. Describe your satisfaction with your vision and the feelings, sensibilities, and passions it elicits.

. . . .

. . . .

. . . .

. . . .

. . . .

. . . .

. . . .

You may feel quite liberated and excited to find this vision for your future. With it you will find a purpose, a direction, a shape to the life you seek. Many leaders give meaning to their lives through the passion they feel for their visions. In his play *Man and Superman*, the British playwright George Bernard Shaw describes how one might feel to live one's vision passionately:

> This is the true joy in life, the being used for a purpose recognized by yourself as a mighty one; the being a force of nature instead of a feverish selfish little clod of ailments and grievances complaining that the world will not devote itself to making you happy. I want to be thoroughly used up when I die, for the harder I work the more I live. I rejoice in life for its own sake. Life is no "brief candle" to me. It is a sort of splendid torch which I have got hold of for the moment, and I want to make it burn as brightly as possible before handing it on to future generations.

Shaw poses a challenge to us: Can we live life to its fullest? Leaders meet that challenge by taking the splendid torch of their lives and with passion and commitment handing the essence of their visions to others, lighting the way for those they wish to lead.

Visions Engage Others

When leaders passionately commit to a shining vision, they inspire others to join them in creating the future. In Chapter 3 we discussed the threat to our planet from global warming and mentioned former Vice President Gore as a leader who addressed these dangers and urged others to resonate with his vision to save the planet. In March 2007, leaders of the European Union met and created a vision that, by 2020, the world will have

- cut greenhouse gas emissions by 20 percent from 1990 levels;
- obtained 20 percent of primary energy from renewable sources, up from 6 percent in 2005;
- reduced energy consumption by 20 percent from 2007 levels.

These may seem modest goals, but the EU leaders hope their passionate commitment to them will draw the United States, China, India, and other countries to an agreement on broad international action to replace the Kyoto Protocol (which is set to expire in 2012) when they meet at the UN Conference on Climate Change in Copenhagen in 2010.

This ability of leaders to draw others to them, as the EU leaders for environmental change are attempting to do worldwide, can be effective if they passionately articulate a vision. When leaders find a vision that is uniquely their own, yet speaks to the real needs and goals of others, they have the power to resonate with the visions of others and inspire them to take action.

Your Organizational Vision—An Exercise

True leaders are responsible for creating visions for the people and organizations they touch. It doesn't matter what job they have or what organizational level they inhabit: They know they must have a vision and communicate it powerfully so that it will guide future accomplishments and achieve success.

Consider, for example, the following vision statements written by two leaders at Apple Computers. They each led the same organization at different times in its history.

> "We will make the computer usable, affordable and available to everyone." (*Steven Jobs*)
> "To make a contribution to the world by making tools that advance humankind." (*John Scully*)

Notice the subtle differences in focus, emphasis, and intention. Your challenge in this exercise is to define, through very careful choice of words, a vision statement for an organization: where you work, where you are studying, where you volunteer, or where you are creating a project. In choosing this organization, make sure that it is one to which you would like to make a contribution, and place yourself in the future to allow your vision to emerge.

To begin, think about the organization as a whole. It may be that in your role you see only a small piece of the entire enterprise. If so, expand your view to include the entire organization—that is, all the people and all the functions that are outside the borders of your daily experience, but are related to your organization in some way.

As you respond to the questions below, let your ideas and wishes flow. Do not censor yourself. Allow the poet and the dreamer who live inside of you to emerge. When you have answered all of the questions, you will be able to write a clear, compelling, and simple vision statement that communicates exactly your wishes for the future of your organization.

Questions to Consider

A. What is it about your organization that is unique, special, and original?

. . . .

. . . .

. . . .

. . . .

. . . .

. . . .

. . . .

B. What are the values that shape your priorities for the future, and how are they expressed in your organization?

. . . .

. . . .

. . . .

. . . .

. . . .

. . . .

. . . .

C. What do your colleagues, as well as customers, clients, and others whom you serve, need and want from the future?

. . . .

. . . .

. . . .

. . . .

. . . .

. . . .

. . . .

D. What would enable you to feel completely committed to and proud of your association with this organization?

. . . .

. . . .

. . . .

. . . .

. . . .

. . . .

. . . .

E. What changes would allow you to personally and passionately commit to your organization for the next five to ten years?

. . . .

. . . .

. . . .

. . . .

. . . .

. . . .

. . . .

F. How would you demonstrate your passion and commitment so that others will join you in this endeavor?

. . . .

. . . .

. . . .

. . . .

. . . .

. . . .

. . . .

Now that you have answered these threshold questions, you can begin clarify and expand your vision for the organization. The following steps will support you in this effort.

Steps to Consider

A. Find a comfortable place at home or in your office where you have the privacy to think and dream. Some people like to think about the future in a quiet natural setting such as a garden or a glen. Others work best over a cup of cappuccino or Earl Grey tea in a noisy coffeehouse. Select the spot that will best enable you to write a vision for your future.

B. Clear your mind of obstacles. Let go of current realities. Avoid telling yourself that your ideas are unrealistic, foolish, silly, or embarrassing. Allow yourself to go as far as possible into your imagination! The time for realism will come later. Now is the time for bold dreams!

C. There are many ways you can choose to express your creativity. You may want to speak your thoughts out loud to yourself or to a friend. You may want to sit quietly and write them down. You may want to sketch or paint a picture. Or you may want to just close your eyes and dream.

D. Try to picture your organization five or ten years in the future, and consider these questions:

- What are the main characteristics of the international environment that will influence your organization ten years from now?
- How does your organization fit into this environment?
- What will your organization contribute to external challenges?
- How do others view your organization?

- How does it feel to live inside this future organization?
- What does the physical plant look like?
- How is your office designed?
- How many people work there?
- What is the attitude toward work of those connected to the enterprise?
- How might you characterize their spirit?
- What kinds of relationships do they have with each other?
- What are the special products and services offered by this organization?
- On the whole, how would you like your organization to be viewed as an employer and a contributor to society?

E. As your vision begins to unfold, capture it in writing in the space below or on your computer, or speak it into a tape recording, or draw it on a large sheet of paper. You may want to present your ideas to someone else or ask that person to help you take notes to capture your ideas. As you vision becomes clearer, develop it, let it expand, and watch it fill your mind until it is compelling, concise, and complete.

Your Vision for Your Organization

. . . .

. . . .

. . . .

. . . .

. . . .

. . . .

. . . .

. . . .

. . . .

. . . .

. . . .

. . . .

. . . .

. . . .

. . . .

. . . .

. . . .

. . . .

. . . .

. . . .

. . . .

. . . .

. . . .

. . . .

A vision is a living document. As a leader, you may want to elicit feedback and involve colleagues in reviewing and revising it. Your vision can only improve by being tested, especially by those you want to lead to a new place. If you are part of a team, ask the other members to share their visions. Look for commonalities among all the vision statements and identify major differences. Negotiate these differences to create a shared vision that everyone can accept and enjoy.

When you communicate your vision to others, do not present your ideas as being the "right" ones or the *only* ones they should consider. Instead, as a leader, you can inspire them to create their *own* images of the future and to find their place in yours, as you find your place in theirs.

When we picture a leader who is engaged in creating a personal vision and committing to it with passion, we imagine a young Barack Obama. We see him in the midst of confusion about his race, his identity, and what the future might hold as he wrestles with turmoil in his family. We are inspired by the courage he exhibited, even as a child, in overcoming the many obstacles in his life. We picture him as having a passionate commitment to a personal vision of himself as the president of the United States.

Your potential to be a leader is exactly the same as that of President Obama and all the great leaders in today's world, and you are entitled to dare to dream of the life you want and to claim it by living your vision.

Creating a Vision for Your Life—An Exercise

Your personal vision is alive and waiting for you. Even when you may not recognize it, this vision is there, inside your heart and mind, and we invite you to follow the guided imagery process described in the next section to discover within it the wishes for your life.

The instructions that follow will allow you to completely relax so you will hear your inner voice and have access to your deepest dreams. If you are working with a partner, ask him or her to read the instructions aloud and lead you through the process. After you have completed the exercise, you can switch and lead your partner to create a vision.

If you are working alone, read the instructions and then close your eyes and repeat them to yourself. Our purpose is to encourage you to relax and let go of any thoughts or feelings that may obstruct your vision from your consciousness.

Steps in Guided Imagery Process

Sit in a comfortable position with your back supported by a chair and your feet firmly planted on the floor. [Pause.] Good.

Uncross your legs and hands and rest your hands on your lap. [Pause.] Good.

Gently let your eyelids become heavy and let them close. Take several deep and easy breaths and slowly release them. [Pause.] With each breath let your body release any tensions. [Pause.] Good.

Notice sounds or movements in the room and release your attention from them. [Pause.] Good.

Release any thoughts you are having. [Pause.] Good.

Release any emotions you are feeling. [Pause.] Good.

Let any pictures from the past drift out of your mind. [Pause.] Good.

Now that you are sitting comfortably in your chair, release any remaining tensions, thoughts, emotions, and pictures from your past. [Pause.] Good.

Focus on your feet and legs. Release any tension in your feet and legs and relax. [Pause.] Good.

Focus your attention on your abdomen and lower body. Release any tension in your abdomen and lower body and relax. [Pause.] Good.

Focus your attention on your chest, shoulders, and arms. Release any tension in your chest, shoulders, and arms and relax. [Pause.] Good.

Focus your attention on your neck, head, and face. Release any tension in your neck, head, and face and relax. [Pause.] Good.

Now that you are fully relaxed, you will remain in a peaceful place. [Pause.] Good.

Let any visions of your future drift into your consciousness. Let any of your dreams, wishes, hopes, and longings come into your mind and your body. [Pause.] Excellent.

Picture your deepest dreams, wishes, hopes, and longings for the kind of person you would most like to be in your future. [Pause.] Good.

Picture the life you would most like to be living in your future. [Pause] Great.

Tell yourself words you would like to hear from others when they talk about you and your life. [Pause.] Excellent.

Imagine yourself feeling completely happy and being fulfilled. [Pause] Great.

Notice what contributes to your happiness and fulfillment. [Pause.] Good.

Stay with the images, feelings, and thoughts that come to you in your vision and enjoy them, relish them, and thank them for visiting you. [Pause] Great.

Let a few minutes pass and begin to feel the back of the chair as it supports your body and feel the floor under your feet. [Pause.] Good.

Begin to return your attention to the present and to the room where you are sitting. [Pause.] Good.

Let your attention turn to the noises in the room. [Pause.] Notice any movements. [Pause.] Good.

As I count to five, you may open your eyes. One. [Pause.] Two. [Pause.] Three. [Pause.] Four. [Pause.] Five. [Pause.] Open your eyes, and say hello to someone in the room. Thank you.

Now that you are relaxed and comfortable and have found your personal vision, you may express it in any form that feels natural. You may think about it, talk about it with a partner, write or record it in a narrative, draw or sculpt it, or use any other form of expression that feels comfortable.

Creative leaders vary in the ways they develop their visions. Some focus on what they think is absolutely necessary to have for themselves and others. Once they know what they want, they put their mind to it and communicate exactly what it is.

Other creative leaders take a different approach. They slog through many ideas and they draft and redraft possibilities while circling around the topic until the vision is born. These leaders begin over and over again until they find what they want to say and how best to say it.

You may enjoy either approach; try both or find a wholly different one. The following questions will guide you in discovering a full and complete personal vision regarding seven different aspects of your life:

1. Self

Start by imagining yourself in the future and living your full potential, demonstrating all your talents, enjoying your strengths, being in your prime, and functioning at your peak. What are your qualities? How do you feel about yourself? What are you doing? How are you living? What brings you joy and happiness?

. . . .

. . . .

. . . .

. . . .

. . . .

. . . .

. . . .

2. Health

Imagine how healthy you can be. Envision your emotional, physical, mental, and spiritual health. Describe all these aspects of your health and then picture the activities and thoughts that will help you achieve and maintain good health.

. . . .

. . . .

. . . .

. . . .

. . . .

. . . .

. . . .

3. Relationship

Picture the person with whom you have your closest relationship. Imagine ideal conversations and activities with that person. What do you hear, see, and feel? What do you give to this person? How do you contribute to each other?

. . . .

. . . .

. . . .

. . . .

. . . .

. . . .

. . . .

4. Family

Include your family members in your vision of yourself. Notice their health and well-being. What is most satisfying about your relationship with each of them? How are you contributing to one another? What is your greatest source of joy within your family?

. . . .

. . . .

. . . .

. . . .

. . . .

. . . .

. . . .

5. Work Life

Consider the vision you have created for your organization and focus on your work. How can you improve the quality of your day-to-day work life? How can you demonstrate your values more explicitly and powerfully? What gives you the greatest satisfaction? What rewards are you receiving? What is the nature of your contribution?

. . . .

. . . .

. . . .

. . . .

. . . .

. . . .

. . . .

6. Community

How might individuals, families, schools, and social institutions in your community benefit from your talents? What can you give to those in need? How satisfying and rewarding will you feel about your social contributions? Picture how you can truly make a difference.

. . . .

. . . .

. . . .

. . . .

. . . .

. . . .

. . . .

7. Enriching Activities

Consider your hobbies, adventures, and volunteer commitments. How might you make these activities more enjoyable and fulfilling? What activities do you treasure more than others? What do you bring to them? What do they contribute to your life?

. . . .

. . . .

. . . .

. . . .

. . . .

. . . .

. . . .

These questions cover a broad spectrum of your life. After you have thought about those that have meaning for you, consider how all the aspects of your life fit together into an integrated vision of the whole. Are there some elements that are in conflict with one another? Can you see your vision as a coherent whole? What parts are fragmented and disjointed? Does your vision please and inspire you? Does it touch and inspire others when you share it with them? Is your vision worthy of your commitment and passion? In the space provided here, or in any other place with any other mode of expression or in any other format you choose, create a complete vision for your personal life.

Your Vision for Yourself

. . . .

. . . .

. . . .

. . . .

. . . .

. . . .

. . . .

. . . .

. . . .

. . . .

. . . .

. . . .

. . . .

. . . .

. . . .

. . . .

. . . .

. . . .

. . . .

. . . .

. . . .

. . . .

. . . .

. . . .

. . . .

Living Your Vision: A Leader's Challenge

A continuing challenge faced by most leaders is to have the courage to *live* their visions. The American historian Dr. John Hope Franklin, whose landmark book *From Slavery to Freedom: A History of African-Americans* altered the prevailing understanding of the history of our country, is an excellent example of a leader who lived his vision.

Franklin had a vision of a society in which all people were accepted and valued. When the brilliant attorney Thurgood Marshall, who led the precedent-setting legal battles to win civil rights for all people, assembled a team of lawyers to mount a legal challenge to segregation in a case before the Supreme Court (where Marshall later served as a Justice), he turned to Franklin for his understanding of the phrase "separate but equal," which appeared in the historic case of *Plessey v. Ferguson* and protected and sustained segregation and discrimination. A decade after Marshall had finally won the 1954 Supreme Court decision of *Brown v. Board of Education* with Franklin's assistance, Franklin joined Dr. Martin Luther King Jr. to lead the civil rights demonstrations in Selma, Alabama. Franklin lived his vision by changing the legal basis for school integration, by transforming the teaching of history in the United States, and by being a first-hand participant in the struggle to realize his powerful dreams.

When leaders communicate their visions with passion, trust flows from followers. Leaders who live their visions increase their self-regard and the regard of others by being in touch with a deeper form of self-knowledge. As you create, embrace, and live your vision, you will discover that it leads you back to your true self, to the place from which you started. Pablo Picasso wrote about this discovery: "I wanted to be a painter and I ended up as Picasso. I began as an artist and I ended up Picasso." Take a moment to consider how your vision can return you to the person you truly are, right now, in this moment. Notice how doing so makes you feel whole and complete. This is the gift your vision offers to you: the power to communicate the person you are, and the ability to share your authentic self with others who matter to you and to your life.

6 Communicating with Meaning: Competency Four

The words we use to describe our conflicts reflect hidden assumptions about our opponents, ourselves, and the meaning of the conflict itself. Our words shape our expectations, limit our interactions and determine our actual relationships. The language we use when we are in conflict reveals our secret biases, limitations, fears, and even how we imagine solutions. Everyone in conflict creates a unique language to describe their experience. Their choice of words reveals what the conflict means to them, how they see their opponents, and how they intend to interact with them.

In other words, each of us has a choice. We can talk about our conflicts as experiences that imprison us, as battles, as opportunities to learn, or as fascinating journeys. Our communications then shape how our conflict unfolds. More importantly, by changing how we communicate, we automatically change now to resolve our conflicts and to learn from them.

—**Kenneth Cloke**
The Crossroads of Conflict: Journey to the Heart of Dispute Resolution

WORDS CAN DETERMINE OUR EXPERIENCES AND REVEAL WHAT we think, feel, and want—not only when we are in conflict, as Ken Cloke so wisely observes, but in every part of our lives, in every encounter, even in every conversation we have with ourselves. Leaders apply this truth about communication when they articulate their visions and when they seek to make their intentions known. They are conscious of the language they use to win the enthusiasm and endorsement they need to realize the dreams they hold dear.

There is a wonderful story that makes this point so well. It is about the first meeting between Orson Welles and Franklin Delano Roosevelt, in which the president graciously told the talented young actor: "You know, Mr. Welles, you are the greatest actor in America." "Oh, no, Mr. President," Welles replied. "You are." These two talented men were masters of communication in the relatively new medium of radio, and each used their charm, wit, and charisma to win their audiences. Roosevelt reassured a fearful nation with his compelling "Fireside Chats"; Welles stirred the same nation to panic with his fanciful description of a Martian invasion of New Jersey in his infamous "War of the Worlds" broadcast. Both men skillfully used theatrical props as well—Welles with his rakish hats, FDR with his signature cape and cigarette holder—to create dashing images. Seemingly without effort they reached out, making their audiences essential to, even determinative of, their greatness.

Leaders are obviously skilled writers and speakers, but, even more important, they excel in person-to-person exchanges. They let colleagues know they've been heard and are committed to give-and-take with them to discover the truth. A good example of a masterful communicator is former *New York Times* editor-in-chief R. W. Apple Jr., whose name was synonymous with quality journalism. Soon after his death, Calvin Trillin, a columnist who knew him well, profiled Apple's talents as a communicator in a *New Yorker* article ("Newshound: The Triumphs, Travels and Movable Feasts of R. W. Apple Jr.," September 20, 2003):

> To characterize the great man's speaking style, collectors of Apple stories often use the phrase "holding forth," although he is also, truth be told, someone who takes in just about everything everyone else in the conversation says and files it away in what Morley Safer, of CBS, who has been a friend of Apple's since they were in Vietnam together, calls "that Palm Pilot of a brain he has."

On the whole, what Apple says while holding forth is considered by his friends worth listening to. The way Ben Bradlee, the former editor of the *Washington Post*, puts it is "I'd like to hear Apple on almost any subject, reserving the right to tell him he's full of shit."

When leaders communicate with meaning, they challenge old conventions, suggest new directions, provide inspiring visions, and advocate innovative ways of doing things.

Great Leaders Are Great Communicators—A Chart

How many times have you wanted a leader to "tell the truth" or "let it all out" or "tell it like it is" or "come clean"? When leaders eliminate uncertainty, their followers feel better about themselves, see a better future, want to join them, and discover who they truly are. If you identify great communicators and note how they choose their words, use their body language, carefully manage their facial expressions, and select the perfect props to reach others, you will be able to develop these skills in your own style to communicate with meaning.

On the chart below, indicate the names of those whom you consider to be brilliant communicators. Select people you know personally or those you admire from a distance. Then note the skills and talents they have that work their magic. When you have completed your observations, share them with colleagues and add their insights to broaden your views.

GREAT COMMUNICATORS   THEIR COMMUNICATION TALENTS

1. . . . .

. . . .

. . . .

. . . .

2. ....

....

....

....

3. ....

....

....

....

4. ....

....

....

....

5. ....

....

....

....

You may notice that the good communicators on your chart span a number of fields, roles, and periods of history and yet many have similar talents. Certain skills are common among successful communicators. Now take a look at your own communication skills. What might you change to communicate powerfully enough to achieve your dreams?

Leaders Communicate and Others Join Them

Leaders develop themselves as events require their talents, wisdom, and action. Abigail Adams, who, as the wife of the early U.S. president John Adams, was a superb communicator as well as a loyal presidential advisor and a shrewd analyst of leadership. She wrote to her son John Quincy Adams in 1780, when he followed his father to become president of the United States: "These are the hard times in which a genius would wish to live. Great necessities call forth great leaders." She understood that simple men could become great leaders by meeting the demands of their times.

Our Founding Fathers also knew that to be effective they had to bring the populace with them as they created a new country. Washington, Jefferson, Adams, Franklin, Madison, and Hamilton come immediately to mind, and it is with awe that we realize such a powerful group of great men shared the stage of history at the same time and responded with vision, communication and commitment to produce a new country.

Leaders who create themselves from humble beginnings, as these men did, know that others must join in their endeavors if they themselves are to succeed. Former President Clinton understood this quality of leadership and demonstrated it when he accepted his party's nomination the first time around. In his speech he movingly spoke of there being "no *them*, only *us*," and if we were to conduct a content-analysis of great political speeches we'd find a wealth of skillfully brandished plural pronouns. Winston Churchill's statement that "*we* shall fight on" in the face of the German blitz is a classic example, which he repeated later in reflecting that this moment in the history of his country was "*our* finest hour." Martin Luther King Jr., a speaker of rare power, moved millions with his gifts as a communicator, and he inspired even those who disagreed with his dream to join his efforts.

Our colleague Howard Gardner, a Harvard University professor of psychology and education, makes an important distinction between leaders who have a direct and visible impact on followers and those who have a more subtle and indirect effect. In his book *Leading Minds*, he points out that indirect leadership differs from direct and immediate leadership but can be a powerful alternative. Al Gore's history as a leader provides a good example of Gardner's distinction. As vice president of the United States under Bill Clinton, Gore had the potential for authority of a direct leader. However, Gore chose a different path: His impact and lasting contribution as a leader came from his commitment to save our planet's environment. He worked behind the scenes in an indirect role with his book, film, and persistent advocacy for sound environmental policy. As you develop your own leadership capacity, you might consider whether you want to take a direct or an indirect role. Either way, be sure to choose a communication style that is appropriate to the type of leadership you want to demonstrate.

Making Communication Meaningful

Sometimes we falsely assume that successful communication rests on the *content* of what we say. For example, have you ever been in a taxi and found the driver did not speak your language? When you realize he has not understood a word of what you said, you start shouting the same instructions, and when that doesn't work, you wave your hands wildly and repeat what he does not understand, over and over again. Have you ever tried to communicate with an unruly adolescent and found that you are using the same unsuccessful techniques, and have never gotten through? These disappointing attempts flounder on the assumption that communication has just one component, and that is the content of what we say, and we ignore that there is more to it than that.

Elements of Meaningful Communication—A Chart

As shown in this diagram, the elements of meaningful communication are the *speaker*, the *message*, the *medium*, the *listener*, and *feedback*. The entire communication is held together and given meaning by *context*. Recall our earlier discussion of the success and significance of President Roosevelt's masterful "Fireside Chats." The *context* for his programs of talks was the turmoil produced by the Great Depression and the fear of the threat of World War II, which not only

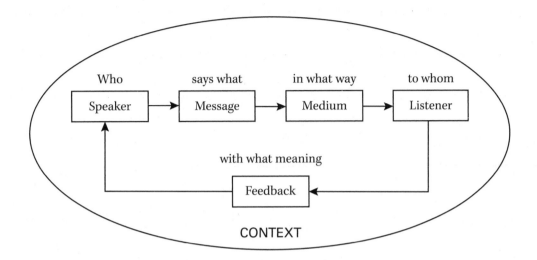

shaped his communications but also enhanced the receptivity of his listeners to his messages of security and strength.

Too often, in planning our communications, we focus on what we *want* to say rather than on the person to *whom* the communication is directed. When communicating, leaders keep in mind the interests, needs, concerns, and priorities of their listeners, so that the content of their intended message is received. The "great communicator," President Ronald Reagan, was a master at speaking to the concerns of those he wished to reach. He probed his staff, questioned the public, and threaded his communications with references to specific individuals and their troubles so he could indicate that he had heard them. He was trusted by many people who felt he asked them relevant questions and came up with answers they wanted to hear. Our colleague Peter Drucker, one of the founders of the field of leadership development, said it well: "The leader of the past knew how to answer. The leader of the future will know how to ask."

Most important, the receptivity of a message is based not only on its substance but on the tone of voice, emotion, and body language used by the sender to deliver it. How many times have you said or thought "I can't hear what you are telling me; your anger is in my way"? Or asked someone to "cool down so I can understand what you want; you're too excited, I can't hear you." Another powerful communicator, Eva Peron, wife and presidential successor of the Argentine dictator Juan Peron, roused the populace to support her presidency after her husband's death not by referring to his social programs or offering political or economic policies but, instead, by expressing emotions many people felt with a strong tone of voice and pleading body language. In this way, she communicated the strength of her ability to hold a position no woman had dared to occupy before her.

In today's intense communication environment there is a plethora of media to carry your messages. The array of choices is intimidating and almost overwhelming! You might personally deliver your message, hold a face-to-face meeting, send a quick e-mail, Twitter, write a "snail mail" letter, post a blog or message on Facebook, create a video for YouTube, schedule a formal assembly, or perhaps even devise a new medium to carry your message in the hope that it can be received.

Integrating the Elements of Communication—An Exercise

When all elements of communication—speaker, message, medium, listener, and feedback as well as context—are in sync, leaders communicate, make themselves known, and discover new ideas and commitments. In this exercise you will strengthen your leadership skills to be more successful in communicating with meaning.

Questions to Consider

Speaker: Take a closer look at yourself as a communicator. What is your preferred communication style? What meaning do you intend to communicate? How are you planning to get your message across? How will it make a difference? What will reinforce your communication to make it successful?

. . . .

. . . .

. . . .

. . . .

. . . .

. . . .

. . . .

Message: What is the most important content of your message? Is it an explicit message, or is it more indirect? What is its deeper meaning in terms of its significance to your goals, your life, your thoughts, and your feelings?

. . . .

. . . .

. . . .

. . . .

. . . .

. . . .

. . . .

Medium: Through what medium will you most effectively communicate your message? Will you make a personal visit, hold a conversation on the telephone, or conduct an exchange on the Internet? Will you call a meeting, write a letter, sing, draw, dance, or dramatize your message? Will you send your message as a list of points, a narrative or will you use another form of presentation appropriate to your meaning?

. . . .

. . . .

. . . .

. . . .

. . . .

. . . .

. . . .

Listener: Who is the intended receiver of your message? Do you want to reach one person, many people, an organization, a community? What do you want to know about your potential listener? How can you find out? What questions would you like to ask to shape your message and increase the chances of it being received?

. . . .

. . . .

. . . .

. . . .

. . . .

. . . .

. . . .

Feedback: What would you like to know from the listener that will help you modify your message so that it can be more fully received? How will you request feedback?

. . . .

. . . .

. . . .

. . . .

. . . .

. . . .

Context: What is the larger context for your communication? What is the context of your relationship with the potential listener? What context supports your message? How do you plan to respond to any changes in the context of your communication?

. . . .

. . . .

. . . .

. . . .

. . . .

. . . .

. . . .

This analysis can give you guidelines for making your communications more meaningful to yourself and your listener. Consider your responses as you return to the communication diagram above, and write the specifics for your intended message, name the medium you wish to use, identify the listener you want to reach, describe the feedback you would find useful, and indicate the context for the entire communication. What insights can you gather in creating and viewing this diagram? How can you use your new ideas to make your communications more meaningful?

A very powerful communicator whom we admire is the former secretary general of the United Nations, Kofi Annan. When he led a peace mission to a perilous and bloody Kenya in 2008 and was joined by Graca Machel, the wife of Nelson Mandela, and Benjamin Mkapa, the former president of Tanzania, they tried to mediate between the two rivals for the presidency of the country, both of whom were leading violent struggles. Annan began each of the several meetings with opposing and warlike factions by inviting a delegate from each side to lead a prayer, and after eleven stormy encounters he chose an unusual prayer from Kenya's national anthem and delivered it himself:

Let all with one accord
In common bond united
Build this nation together
And the glory of Kenya

He continued with a further prayer: "Lord . . . May you lead them that they may unite in a common bond not only to build their nation together but now also to build their nation together. Amen."

Annan skillfully used all the elements of communication to achieve his goal, and many leaders, like him, understand that every gesture, every word, every nuance is key to communicating their intention, commitment, and connection to those they wish to reach.

Media Shapes Communication

In many cases, leaders find their communications filtered through the media. As leaders try to keep up with the rapidly expanding number of outlets for their communications, they discover that the media they choose will shape the perceptions of followers they are trying to reach. They wonder: Will their messages that are accessed on a Blackberry be viewed differently from those read in the printed pages of the *New York Times*? Is a politician's vision reported on the news-oriented pages of a local paper perceived differently from the same vision presented on the op-ed page? Do viewers of television talk shows have a different relationship with political candidates than listeners of radio talk shows? Does the stature of the interviewer asking the questions alter people's perception of the candidates? What is the role of today's news photographers in influencing how we visualize leaders? Are the words and thoughts of popular bloggers viewed as better sources of information about a leader than the full text of the leader's speech?

To understand modern leadership we need a much deeper appreciation of the power of these media, given all their uses and the biases they trigger on a global scale.

Aligning with Others Through Meaning—An Exercise

The promise made by Walt Disney at the Disney Epcot Center in Orlando, Florida—"If you can dream it, you can do it"—beckons the Don Quixote in all of us. Yet, as Cervantes' hero warns, believing in one's dreams is not enough. Intoxicating visions and noble intentions will come to naught if they are not communicated in a way that inspires enthusiasm in others to make them real. As you review the following communication qualities of leaders, indicate how you will improve your own communications so that you can align others to join you in realizing your vision, dreams, and intentions.

1. Unify

Neither leaders nor followers can exist without the other, and when they are in sync, they bring out the best in the other. Leaders create unifying visions, much as described by the brilliant historian Doris Kerns Goodwin when she wrote of President Abraham Lincoln's unifying genius in her Pulitzer Prize–winning history of Lincoln's presidency, *Team of Rivals*:

> Lincoln possessed . . . a profound self-awareness that enabled him to find constructive ways to alleviate sadness and stress. Indeed, when he is compared with his colleagues, it is clear that he possessed the most even-tempered disposition of them all. Time and again, he was the one who dispelled his colleagues' anxiety and sustained their spirits with his gift for storytelling and his life-affirming sense of humor. When resentment and contention threatened to destroy his administration, he refused to be provoked by petty grievances, to submit to jealousy, or to brood over perceived slights. Through the appalling pressures he faced day after day, he retained an unflagging faith in his country's cause.

Your belief in your vision for the future and your unswerving commitment to your values can be sources of unity when you communicate them honestly, directly, and with compassion.

Indicate How You Will Improve Your Communication to More Effectively Unify Others:

. . . .

. . . .

. . . .

. . . .

. . . .

. . . .

. . . .

2. Empathize

Effective leaders empathize with those they wish to reach—and communicate that they are willing to walk in the shoes of others—to create a vision of the future that will realize their desires and dreams. They are careful to let others know they recognize who they are and what they experience in their lives.

Former CBS executive Barbara Corday prized empathy, and described it as an integral part of her approach to leadership:

> I have always been very pleased and happy and proud of the fact that I not only know all the people who work for me, but I know their husbands' and wives' names, and I know their children's names, and I know who's been sick, and I know what to ask. That's what's special to me in a work atmosphere. I think that's what people appreciate, and that's why they want to be there, and that's why they're loyal, and that's why they care about what they're doing.

The experience of empathy can be a liberating one, as you will discover as you take off your blinders and truly experience a connection with another person.

Describe How You Will Increase Your Empathy with Others:

. . . .

. . . .

. . . .

. . . .

. . . .

. . . .

. . . .

3. Partner

Meaningful communications with others occur when leaders hold out a hand to create partnerships for the long haul. Here is how the former CEO of Lucky Stores, Don Ritchey, got across the message that he was a partner with the people who worked for him:

> I think one of the biggest turn-ons for people is to know that their peers and particularly their bosses not only know they're there but know pretty intimately what they're doing and are involved with them on almost a daily basis, that it's a partnership, that you're really trying to run this thing well together, that if something goes wrong our goal is to fix it, not see who we can nail.

Truly being a partner, in a jointly shared endeavor, calls for you to communicate your questions, concerns, and suggestions with an open mind.

Indicate How You Will Be a More Effective Partner with Others:

. . . .

. . . .

. . . .

. . . .

. . . .

. . . .

. . . .

4. Inspire with Metaphors

Leaders use metaphors to include others in realizing their goals. For Charles Darwin, the metaphor was a branching tree of evolution on which he traced the rise of various species. William James viewed mental processes as a stream or river. John Locke focused on the falconer, whose release of the bird symbolized his "own emerging view of the creative process." These leaders stepped away from their ordinary professional language to use unusual and vivid imagery from other fields and other worlds, so that those they wished to reach who did not have their training or sophistication could understand their ideas.

When Frank Dale became president and publisher of the *Los Angeles Herald-Examiner,* Los Angeles's only afternoon newspaper in the 1980s, a bloody ten-year labor-management conflict was just ending. Dale had to use the back door to get to his office on the first day because the front door had been barred. This is the way Dale used a metaphor to meaningfully communicate that his leadership brought a new day to the paper:

> The lobby had been barricaded for over eight years. There was tremendous strife, people were killed, employees were killed and indeed, . . . eventually some employees . . . said to each other over a beer one night: "We gotta quit shooting each other." And so, on a peace platform, they got the employees to vote for a settlement and eventually got the right to bargain.
>
> I called the people on duty at the time around the desk in an informal setting—I had no one to introduce me. . . . I did it myself so that I would be right there and without any forethought at all I said, "Maybe the first thing we ought to do is open up the front door." Everybody stood up and cheered. Grown men and women cried. That was a symbol, you see, that barricade was

a symbol of defeat, of siege. And "let the sun in" was what I was saying. . . . And then I attempted to introduce myself again, thanked them for preserving the opportunity that I had been asked to take advantage of. Which is really what they did—when I let the sunshine in.

Indicate How You Will Inspire Others Through Metaphor:

. . . .

. . . .

. . . .

. . . .

. . . .

. . . .

. . . .

5. Encourage Transparency and Candor

Genuine leaders encourage transparency, candor, and honest sharing of information with colleagues in all their endeavors. By doing so, they create organizations that draw on goodwill and weather scrutiny when things go wrong. Their organizations have little to fear from media critics or dissatisfied bloggers, because the leaders acknowledge their mistakes in a timely fashion.

As the 2008 financial crisis increased the role of government oversight, leaders of the Obama administration demanded new standards of candor, honesty, and openness. Following the Obama example, the Whole Foods grocery chain has gone a long way toward achieving an open and transparent organization. The CEO, John Mackey, described their "no secrets" policy in a recent interview:

> We post every employee's pay. The rationale for this and other practices we hope will be egalitarian and transparency-related (including limiting executive pay to a modest multiple of everyone else's) is my belief in the "shared

fate" of all who work at Whole Foods. Transparency is a highly valued element in our culture, and we hope it contributes to our frequent appearance at the top of lists of best places to work.

Describe How You Will Encourage Transparency and Candor:

. . . .

. . . .

. . . .

. . . .

. . . .

. . . .

Leaders who successfully pursue these five goals communicate with meaning and motivate others to become leaders in their own right. They unify listeners with one another by sharing a compelling vision. They let colleagues and followers know they empathize with their attempts to overcome obstacles. They inspire listeners by embroidering their communications with stories, metaphors, and stirring examples. They are committed to openness and candor, and they model their beliefs by engaging in forthright, direct communications.

Leaders Resolve Conflicts

"Curse you! May you live in interesting times" goes a famous Chinese imprecation. No one would argue that we live and work in interesting, albeit difficult and conflicted, times. Change is now a constant, and the conflicts that inevitably accompany it create demands for mediative leadership. The growing mistrust of business and government, the emerging global recession, the aftermath of September 11, the wars in Pakistan, Afghanistan, and Iraq, the threat of catastrophic environmental changes, and increasingly fierce corporate competition offer urgent demands for leaders to guide us toward significant resolutions of conflicts on a worldwide scale.

Internal organizational conflicts as well as secrecy that exploits differences for gain further jeopardize our fragile economy. Indeed, we are now faced with the discouraging fact that decision makers fail to listen to and learn from the communications in their own organizations. As early as 2004, more than two dozen high-ranking executives of Freddie Mac warned their chief executive, Richard Syron, about the economic failure that would eventually result from the rush to lend sub-prime mortgages. Rather than directly face conflict and engage in complex communications to consider diverse points of view, Syron rejected this information, which otherwise might have protected his organization from the damage it caused by engaging in risky financial and lending practices.

Another startlingly negative example of organizational cultures based on secrecy, dishonesty, and aversion to open conflict communication emerged years earlier, during the Enron Corporation scandal. At Enron, simply talking about what was actually going on was off-limits. As one executive later observed, "You simply didn't want to discuss anything important in front of the water cooler."

These dramatic examples tell us that one of the most difficult things to do in *any* organization is to speak truth to power. In light of this challenge, leaders must create a social architecture that permits, gives license to, and encourages open and honest communications. Without it, many organizations are doomed to failure. The space shuttle *Challenger* disaster is another case in point. Some of those who built the shuttle knew there was a defect in the o-rings included in the structure. The man who reported the problem was fired when he broke with the coercive "groupthink" that was committed to suppressing the truth.

Leaders Communicate to Resolve Conflicts—An Exercise

Traditional power-based and bureaucratic approaches to conflict often suppress useful information, block effective communication, and discourage those who can use their disputes to expose what isn't working and set things right.

The philosophy of leadership we endorse, by contrast, encourages open communication and the building of organizational cultures where honest expression of conflicts and candid discussion of differences lead to resolution. As you review the elements of this philosophy below, think of a conflict you have that is related to each element and identify how you might improve your communication to resolve that conflict.

A concept of *humanity* based on increased understanding of our complex, multilayered, and shifting needs is replacing an oversimplified, mechanical idea of who we are and what we need and desire.

THE CONFLICT   COMMUNICATIONS TO RESOLVE IT

. . . .

. . . .

. . . .

. . . .

A concept of *power* based on collaboration, reason, and synergy is replacing a model of power that is steeped in adversarial assumptions, leading to violence, coercion, and threats.

THE CONFLICT   COMMUNICATIONS TO RESOLVE IT

. . . .

. . . .

. . . .

. . . .

A concept of *values* based on humanistic-democratic ideals is replacing a depersonalized, bureaucratic value system that regards wealth, status, and rules-driven values as being more important than people, relationships, and value-driven rules.

THE CONFLICT   COMMUNICATIONS TO RESOLVE IT

. . . .

. . . .

. . . .

. . . .

A concept of *conflict* based on personal and organizational learning, creative problem solving, collaborative negotiation, and mediation is replacing an approach to conflict that avoids, suppresses, and hides it and prevents us from addressing the underlying reasons that gave rise to it, and from using the conflict to foster personal and organizational improvement.

THE CONFLICT   COMMUNICATIONS TO RESOLVE IT

. . . .

. . . .

. . . .

. . . .

As leaders, we must attempt to apply this new philosophy to cope with rapid, uncertain change, grapple with global interdependence, search for meaningful relations, and deal with the tensions that aggravate social strains, psychological uncertainty, and chronic conflicts. The ability of successful leaders at every level in an organization to foster and promote honest communication is fundamental to creating cultures of resolution and peace in which self-examination is valued and people freely offer their honest reactions. In this environment, differences in perceptions, habits, languages, and styles are valued; indeed, they are plumbed for unique and diverse contributions.

143

Leaders generate trust so that employees feel comfortable communicating openly, honestly, and empathetically. In doing so, they encourage addressing even serious conflicts, so that everyone becomes skilled in turning these conflicts into opportunities for improvements in communications, relationships, and outcomes.

Communicating Your Vision—An Exercise

Your vision can be a powerful force for change and conflict resolution if you communicate it to others in a way that it is accessible and inspiring. The next step you can take as a leader is to plan how to communicate your vision to others.

In this exercise, we ask you to plan how you will communicate your vision so that you successfully reach others and move them to trust you and to join you in acting on your intentions. Your challenge will be to communicate powerfully and inspirationally so that others can easily embrace and support your ideas and your intentions.

In presenting your vision, you can use a drawing, a song, a poem, a skit, a narrative, or any other form you choose. In planning your presentation, think about the members of your audience and their needs, their own communication styles, their concerns, and their hopes and dreams. Look for ways to fire them up, reach their hearts, and inspire them to join you in your pursuits.

If you have been working alone, invite a small group of colleagues to assist you. Invite them to hear or see your vision and to discuss it with you. If they have created visions of their own, have them present these to each other. Let them know that you really value their honest reactions.

As others consider your vision, you may want to invite them to suggest changes—and if they do so, avoid being defensive. Invite them to make the vision their own by adding whatever will help them to feel it is theirs. Stay true to your basic principles, but let them rework the language, design the presentation, and suggest the ideas so that more people can support what you intend to achieve.

Sharing your personal vision with others is the next step in the visioning process. If you do not feel ready to present your personal vision to colleagues, share it with family or others who are close to you. Think about how your personal vision compares with your organizational vision. Is there dissonance between the two? If there is a conflict, consider whether you can change your organization or should move on to a new workplace. Ask yourself if your personal vision is as clear and compelling as your organizational vision. Try to incorporate ideas from others into your own personal vision. Ask your friends and family for their reactions and support. Revising and reworking one's personal vision are natural and continual processes for a leader. Think of your vision as a living document, and plan to engage in new ways of communicating it on an ongoing basis.

Now that you have learned to translate your vision into reality, a subsequent step for you as a leader is to learn to build trusting relationships with those who can assist you in realizing this vision. In Chapter 7 you will gain a new leadership competency: maintaining the trust of others through demonstrating your capacity for integrity.

7 Maintaining Trust Through Integrity:
Competency Five

Roosevelt and Churchill became friends under the force of circumstance. . . .
Eleanor [Roosevelt]'s postwar testimony: "I shall never cease to be grateful to
Churchill for his leadership during the war. The real affection, which he had for
my husband and which was reciprocated, he has apparently never lost. The
war would have been harder to win without it, and the two men might not have
gone through it so well if they had not had that personal pleasure in meeting
and confidence in each other's integrity and ability. . . . "

    Though they had their differences—Churchill wanted the British empire to
survive and thrive, Roosevelt largely favored self-determination for colonial
peoples around the world—they cared passionately about the same overarch-
ing truth: breaking the Axis. Victory was the common goal, and only Roosevelt
and Churchill knew the uncertainties that came with ultimate power. . . . To-
gether they preserved the democratic experiment.

    —Jon Meacham
    Franklin and Winston: An Intimate Portrait of an Epic Friendship

HOW DID THESE MEN—DIFFERENT IN TEMPERAMENT, PRIORITIES, and demands from their constituents—trust each other so deeply that they could forge a relationship that empowered Churchill to inspire his tiny nation to be a major bulwark against Nazi power in Europe, and Roosevelt to bring his isolationist country into World War II with full force?

Why did thousands of India's poor march across their country to follow Gandhi in protest of the salt tax, a symbol of colonial power? What was it about Margaret Sanger that emboldened a large number of women who were her contemporaries to break with their husbands and families to adopt birth control? How did Dr. Martin Luther King Jr. inspire thousands of uneducated sharecroppers, tied to the soil of the American South, to risk their lives by registering to vote? What was it about César Chávez that empowered communities of destitute farm workers, who spoke no English, to use their voices to refuse the back-breaking work of picking grapes for less than a living wage, and that motivated middle-class consumers to support them by boycotting grapes and wine for their tables?

Each of these leaders, and many others, marshaled the trust of their followers with their invincible integrity and unswerving commitment to the beliefs they advocated. When leaders create an appealing vision, articulate shared values, and inspire worthwhile goals, trust takes hold. These leaders "walk their talk," and deliver on what they promise, to meet the needs of those they serve. They have a kind of steadiness in difficult times, and when they are under pressure they are not reckless with the trust they have gained. They prove, over and over, that they are on the side of those who follow their ideals.

Leaders Engender Trust—An Exercise

There is no particular technique or easy formula by which leaders learn to build trust; however, trust is given when leaders demonstrate four complex, far-reaching characteristics.

As you review these characteristics, please rate your skills on a scale of 1 to 5 for each of them. *A score of 1* indicates that you are not at the top of your game and want to put energy and focus into developing this characteristic. *A score of 5* signifies that you embody this characteristic and usually demonstrate it in your words and deeds. After you give yourself an honest score, indicate any behaviors you want to change and target any skills you want to improve so as to master this competency and become a more effective leader who is trusted for your integrity.

1. Competence

A foundation of leadership is the capacity to do a job well and perform it with accuracy and skill to achieve success. Leaders do what is required to achieve excellence. They thrive on "the job well done." They also measure their success on mentoring others to become leaders in their own right.

My Rating for This Characteristic

Needs Work   **1**   **2**   **3**   **4**   **5**   **Quite Successful**

Behaviors I Want to Change

. . . .

. . . .

. . . .

. . . .

Skills I Want to Develop

. . . .

. . . .

. . . .

. . . .

2. Congruity

Leaders with integrity live their values. What they do is congruent with what they say and feel. They effectively express their visions and their ethical commitments through their actions, and they do so explicitly and consistently.

My Rating for This Characteristic

Needs Work   **1**   **2**   **3**   **4**   **5**   **Quite Successful**

Behaviors I Want to Change

. . . .

. . . .

. . . .

. . . .

Skills I Want to Develop

. . . .

. . . .

. . . .

. . . .

3. Constancy

Leaders who are recognized for their constancy let others know that in the heat of battle they will watch their backs and fully support them, regardless of the odds against them. They can be counted on to come through with winning strategies.

My Rating for This Characteristic

Needs Work   **1**   **2**   **3**   **4**   **5**   **Quite Successful**

Behaviors I Want to Change

. . . .

. . . .

. . . .

. . . .

Skills I Want to Develop

. . . .

. . . .

. . . .

. . . .

4. Caring

Leaders who are perceived as caring are known to be genuinely concerned about the lives of others. They empathize with those whom they encounter. They are trusted to be responsible for their actions and for the results they produce from their decisions.

My Rating for This Characteristic

Needs Work   **1**   **2**   **3**   **4**   **5**   **Quite Successful**

Behaviors I Want to Change

. . . .

. . . .

. . . .

. . . .

Skills I Want to Develop

. . . .

. . . .

. . . .

. . . .

As lifelong learners, leaders are committed to continually attempting to master the qualities of competence, congruity, constancy, and caring throughout their lives. They place these four characteristics high on their learning agenda. If the same characteristics are important to you, add their mastery to your *Personal Leadership Agenda* and your plans for learning to lead.

Optimism Invites Trust

Unfortunately, limits, constraints, disappointments, and reduced expectations seem to be common in our times. How many of the failures currently reported in the media might have been prevented, avoided, and repaired if the rule of thumb had not been to "get by," "shine it on," or "cover it up." For true leaders, even in this anemic *zeitgeist*, "Yes, We Can" is regarded as much more than just a political slogan. It guides their every effort.

Optimistic leaders have a sixth sense with which they define reality in a compelling way. Rather than falling into sentimentalism or being guilty of painting falsely rosy pictures, these leaders demonstrate *creative pragmatism* and believe in the possibility of redemption for everyone, even in the worst of times. Optimistic leaders have resilience and the ability to generate *creative* options, and they deploy these talents to enroll others in visions of *pragmatic* possibility. Their hardiness has a determination that leads them to refuse to surrender to any difficulties in achieving their goals. They do not let crises control their destiny; rather, they put their trust in the capacity of humankind to prevail.

Leaders who confront today's economic, political and social crises viscerally sense that, to maintain their optimism and encourage others to believe in their worldview, they must build coalitions, engage collaborative partners, and enlist supporters for their dreams.

Far from considering his indeterminate number of years in prison in South Africa as an inexorable defeat, Nelson Mandela turned his imprisonment into an opportunity to develop the skill of winning others to support his vision for his country—a skill that ultimately saved his life. He not only engaged leaders all over the world to demand his release and believe in his leadership but recruited even the unlikeliest prospects to his cause: his own prison guards. Mandela's ability to engage others in his hope and optimism, and to engender trust from those struggling with their own difficulties, is a hallmark of his masterful leadership.

Pragmatic and optimistic leaders who inspire creativity enable others to survive in tough times, or any time. They transform difficulty into possibility as they see beyond conventional limits and inspire their allies to overcome the restrictions of their times.

Trust Contributes to Organizational Effectiveness—An Exercise

Trust is difficult to describe, let alone define; yet we recognize trusted leaders when we see them. Trusted leaders consistently make four distinct contributions to the organizations in which they work, study, and participate. And when they do so, they not only improve the effectiveness of everyone involved but transform the workplace itself.

In this exercise, we describe contributions that trusted leaders make to their organizations. Please review them and indicate how you will expand your abilities as a trusted leader and inspire organizational effectiveness when you attempt to make these contributions to those with whom you work.

1. Vision

Trusted leaders offer clear and inspiring visions to generate a context of shared values and common purposes. These leaders invite colleagues to join them in making their visions real and in integrating them into their work and lives.

Contributions to My Organization That I Can Make with My Vision

. . . .

2. Empathy

Trusted leaders have unconditional empathy for their colleagues. They encourage them to listen deeply to one another. They walk in the shoes of others and let them know they are doing so. They see the world as others see it and make an effort to understand how others arrived at conclusions that may differ from their own.

Contributions to My Organization That I Can Make Through Empathy

. . . .

. . . .

. . . .

3. Consistency

Trusted leaders behave consistently with their values and are true to their commitments. Those with whom they work know where they stand regarding not just the big picture but also specific problems that influence day-to-day events. They clearly express how their views evolved, and they are willing to reconsider their ideas in the face of new evidence.

Contributions to My Organization That I Can Make Through Consistency

. . . .

. . . .

. . . .

. . . .

4. Integrity

The integrity of trusted leaders is unquestionable. They can be counted on to take a stand, encourage a higher moral order, and demonstrate their ethics and values through observable action. They hold themselves and others to account to never deviate from what they know is the right thing to do.

Contributions to My Organization That I Can Make Through Integrity

. . . .

. . . .

. . . .

. . . .

As you identify any valuable contributions you plan to make to your organization, take a moment to consider how you will implement these contributions and what support you will need to follow through.

Leaders Inspire Trust Through Empathy

Visionary leaders' capacity for empathy is a make-or-break quality in attracting followers and building bonds of lasting trust.

When a leader empathizes, they behave differently from when they sympathize. Actually, these two processes are mutually exclusive. Leaders who sympathize focus on their own feelings and we are left with the experience that they are not really interested in us. They seem to be going through the motions. We feel misunderstood or diminished when sympathizers put themselves in a superior position, with comments like "Oh you poor thing, you must be feeling bad (or sad, or upset)." The sympathizer does not even try to find out what we are actually feeling but, instead, projects feelings onto us, never checking to find out what we really feel or if that feeling is true.

Empathizers, by contrast, make no judgments about anyone else or what they may be feeling; rather, they solicit a report about what is going on with them and try to experience the feelings of others as their own. These leaders find a place within themselves that is much like the one they perceive in the other person. They detach from those feelings and recognize them as shared. This detachment does not seem like indifference to us. We feel that they respect us, and they are certain that we are entitled to our own reality. They support and encourage our independence and security. They are secure in their sense of themselves and they are clear about their own emotional boundaries and those of others. Empathetic leaders seek to nurture security through their empathy.

Practicing Empathy—An Exercise

When you successfully empathize with others, you elicit their trust. You do so by making a conscious effort to listen and truly hear and understand what they are saying. Your attention is on them, and you engage in the conversation by

- feeding back to them what you hear them say or see them do;
- asking questions to learn about what they really feel or believe;
- repeating their comments to show you've heard them and are not imposing your ideas;
- understanding their point of view from the inside out, as though it were your own.

Empathetic leaders do not judge the responses of others, or stifle them with preconceived agendas; rather, they listen in silence and give others the opportunity to have their own unique reactions and to feel that they are genuinely heard and known for who they are.

The following case study provides an opportunity for you to practice your skills of empathy. As you read it, observe your reactions to the characters in the story and notice if any of their behaviors, attitudes, or feelings are problematic for you. If you have a hard time empathizing with any of the characters, seek to recognize whether their behaviors and attitudes are familiar to you or remind you of other people whose behaviors are difficult for you to accept. After reading the case study, plan how you might show empathy and coach each of the characters, no matter how you feel about them.

A Case Study

Sarah is a relatively new employee of an advertising company that she joined about six months ago. She is an experienced advertising executive with about twenty years in the business and left a previous agency of her own accord, in search of new challenges and more interesting work. The high-end, highly visible clients of the present company attracted her. She has excellent creative skills, and she was hired as a non-manager to join a team with a new, large, high-stakes client because of her outstanding qualifications. She has a Ph.D. and is quite talented as an artist.

Michael is Sarah's manager. He has been with the agency for ten years and, for three successful years, has been the manager of the team that Sarah recently joined. He is highly respected by their prized client, with whom he has been working for six months. When he joined the agency he was a non-manager, and in subsequent years he has been rapidly promoted up through the ranks. He is valued for his technical expertise and management skills as leader of his team. Michael joined the advertising field shortly after he completed his bachelor's degree and later earned a master's while working full-time at the firm and going to school at night.

When Michael interviewed Sarah for his team, she thought of him as someone she could mentor. She saw him as a young and inexperienced "pup." She considers Michael to be "beneath her" in education, skills, and sophistication. Michael, on the other hand, considers himself Sarah's boss, and he is pleased to have the benefit of her talents on his team and to have a woman join his all-male "crowd."

Sarah and Michael are having trouble getting along with each other and their problems are confusing to each of them. Michael likes Sarah and wonders why she behaves in such a disrespectful way toward him; for example, she often interrupts him in front of the rest of the team, correcting him with what she thinks is "the right approach to take for *this* client." He particularly bristles when she refers to him as being "wet behind the ears" and when she points out her "superiority," which she attributes to her Ph.D. and "having been around that problem millions of times."

At the same time, Sarah is feeling ignored and undervalued by Michael and the rest of the team. She believes that in his eyes her experience is "not worth the paper it is written on," and she resents his sexist attitude when he treats her like "the little woman" and "struts like a he-man" around the shop. She doesn't have anyone she can confide in and feels that the environment "oozes with testosterone." She's never before felt so lonely on a job.

Michael's performance appraisal is scheduled in three weeks, and it will be a "360-degree process" in which he'll be evaluated by everyone who works around him—namely, his team, his client, his direct reports, and his boss. He is nervous about what Sarah will say. He knows his "boys" will give him positive reviews but he is worried that Sarah's assessment will put his bonus in jeopardy. Her opinion really counts with the "higher-ups."

Meanwhile, Sarah has been noticing negative responses to the advertising strategies she has been "pitching" to the "big-bucks" client and is worried about the size of the bonus coming her way in a few weeks. She figures she's spent most of it already and is dreaming of a vacation in Italy if all goes well.

If you are to effectively advise both Michael and Sarah so they will hear each other, be able to mend fences, and not be defensive or resent your intervention, you must begin with empathy. The following questions may help you empathize with each of them and discover ways to understand their predicament and help them find the resolution to their conflict that each of them needs.

Questions to Consider

A. What are Sarah's insecurities and fears? How might you draw her out so that she owns her worries and talks about them? How can you introduce the conversation with her alone, and what questions can you ask?

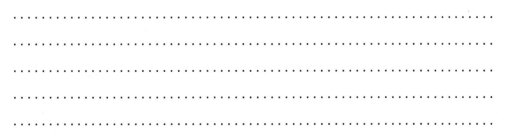

. . . .

. . . .

B. What are Michael's insecurities and fears? How might you draw him out and encourage him to talk about what troubles him so that he is responsible for the actions he took that provoked his problems with Sarah? What introduction can you make to your intervention, and what questions can you ask when you meet with him alone?

. . . .

. . . .

. . . .

. . . .

. . . .

. . . .

. . . .

C. What might Sarah and Michael contribute to each other so that each of them would feel more valued and accepted, and how might you bring them together to share their ideas?

. . . .

. . . .

. . . .

. . . .

. . . .

. . . .

. . . .

D. What does Sarah want from Michael? What does Michael want from Sarah? How can you help them tell each other what they want so that they can hear each other?

. . . .

. . . .

. . . .

. . . .

. . . .

. . . .

. . . .

E. What questions can you ask Sarah and Michael to help them recognize the feelings of the other person?

. . . .

. . . .

. . . .

. . . .

. . . .

. . . .

. . . .

F. What might Sarah do, or say to Michael, to repair their relationship and improve their work together on the team?

. . . .

. . . .

. . . .

. . . .

. . . .

. . . .

. . . .

G. What might Michael do, or say to Sarah, to repair their relationship and improve their work together on the team?

. . . .

. . . .

. . . .

. . . .

. . . .

. . . .

. . . .

H. What might Michael and Sarah do or say to let the team, the client, and the "higher-ups" know that they have repaired their relationship and improved the way they will work together in the future?

. . . .

. . . .

. . . .

. . . .

. . . .

. . . .

. . . .

Leaders often practice empathetic coaching to resolve negative situations and conflicts. If you are part of a team, you may find it worthwhile to role-play a coaching session in which one colleague plays Sarah's part, another plays Michael's, and you play the coach or mediator. In this role, you will want to begin by reflecting on Sarah and Michael's situation, putting yourself in the shoes of each person and identifying a time when you have been in similar situations or had similar feelings.

Alternatively, you may want to find out which team members most dislike or disapprove of Sarah or Michael and then ask them to play their roles, so that they have a chance to feel what it's like to live in the skin of someone they do not like. In this way they can learn to empathize with that person. And if *you* play the role of the person you find most difficult, you will discover a great deal about yourself, including which behaviors or attitudes push your buttons. Doing this task will give you a chance to be an empathetic leader and to see the world from Michael and Sarah's point of view so that you can discover how to help them increase their success on the job.

Stages in Empathetic Coaching

While there is no fixed script for empathetic coaching, there are stages that most empathetic coaches follow to reach success. When you review the seven stages of the coaching process discussed below and apply them to how you might coach Sarah and Michael, or apply them in connection with a real-life coaching situation, you will have a better grasp of how you might become a trusted leader by being an empathetic coach.

1. Introduce the Session

Begin with an introduction by telling Sarah or Michael why you are meeting together and then share your goals for the coaching session. Ask them what they would like to achieve. Assume they are willing to work with you, but also know that one or both may be resistant. You may reduce resistance from them if you let them know that you are not biased toward or against either person.

2. Set the Stage

Create an opportunity for Sarah and Michael to tell you what they think went wrong with their relationship. Begin with the person you feel is "power-down." In this case, Sarah is lower on the hierarchy, and in addition she may feel that she has less power because she is the lone woman in a male-dominant team environment. After she speaks, ask Michael to tell his side of the story. As each person speaks, empathize with the feelings they express. Try to see the situation from the viewpoint of the person speaking, as well as from that of the person listening. As you listen, notice the body language of both the speaker and the listener and understand what the nonverbal signals are telling you. Be sure to ask both people to tell what is on their minds and in their hearts. Remain silent but encouraging with appropriate nods, eye contact, and responsive body gestures.

3. Offer Empathetic Remarks

Let both Sarah and Michael know that you appreciate their situation and the feelings they are having. Summarize what was said and ask questions to go deeper into the *meaning* of each communication. Acknowledge any emotions and let Sarah and Michael know that you empathize with both of them. Do not take personally any anger or defensiveness that they express but, instead, encourage each person to explore the issues and discover whatever feelings lie beneath the anger. Ask them to work together to find a solution that is acceptable to each of them. Create a partnership.

4. Provide Feedback and Engage in Supportive Confrontation

With as much honesty as you can muster, give Sarah and Michael feedback on their behavior and point of view. Your direct observations should help each of them empathize with the other and understand the impact that their behavior has had on the other person. Let Sarah and Michael know, individually, that you have their self-interest at heart and are considering the big picture, including the success of the company and the approval of the client.

Empathy gives you permission to provide what we call "supportive confrontation," which involves telling each person honestly about any problems you have with their negative behavior. Do not protect either of them from learning about themselves through your honest observations: Be direct and, at the same time, come from a supportive place. Ask both of them if they are willing to improve their communications and what they can do differently to make future communications more effective. Encourage each person to empathize with the other and understand why his or her behavior is felt to be upsetting and disruptive.

5. Solicit Reactions

Find out if both Sarah and Michael received and understood your feedback. Hear what they have to say and, even if it is critical, use it as an opportunity to demonstrate how criticism can be accepted in a thoughtful and positive manner. Listen for disappointments, pain, and a sense of failure. Let each person know that you hear their feelings and understand why he or she feels that way.

6. Elicit Changes

Encourage Sarah and Michael to meet and prepare a plan of action. Facilitate their meeting, and encourage them to focus on specifics to improve their relationship and communications. Ask them to describe new behaviors they would like to see in the other person, and those they are willing to offer from themselves. Also ask them to indicate changes they would like to see in the way the team operates and changes they'd like to make in their relationship with the client. Prompt each of them to commit to changing their behaviors immediately and to work together to elicit new behaviors and attitudes from others in the company.

7. Offer Acknowledgments

Thank Sarah and Michael for taking the risk to be open and courageous and willing to change. Empathize with them, and indicate how hard it must have been to honestly observe themselves and to ask for changes from the other person. Encourage each to be more acknowledging of the other and to find small ways of complimenting each other for work well done.

As you continue to develop your leadership skills and take steps to influence the world around you, you will find empathetic coaching to be an effective skill in a variety of settings. You may use these seven steps in any order you choose when a colleague or friend asks for advice, direction, and coaching. Indeed, you might find other colleagues who remind you of Sarah and Michael, and who are locked in struggles with each other. It will seem as if this case study has come true, and you can use your new skills to support the resolution of the conflict by all who may be involved.

Empathy Results in Self-Awareness—An Exercise

Take a moment to reflect on how you felt when you tried to empathize with Sarah and Michael. What about each of them was difficult for you to understand or to empathize with? If you found that either Sarah's or Michael's story pushed your buttons, you may discover that you have some similar unresolved issues with someone in your own life, or even with yourself—issues that you need to work through as you develop as a leader. Leaders understand that it is precisely the most problematic people in their lives who can be their greatest teachers.

If you would like to gain insights into any of your unresolved issues with others and want to increase you capacity to empathize with them, try the steps in the following exercise.

A. Below, make a list of the people at work or at home whom you find difficult and with whom you are unable to empathize.

. . . .

. . . .

. . . .

. . . .

. . . .

. . . .

. . . .

B. For each person, list the attributes or behaviors you find most disagreeable, including those with which you can't empathize.

. . . .

. . . .

. . . .

. . . .

. . . .

. . . .

. . . .

C. Review the characteristics you've indicated above and notice any similarities among the people on your list. Determine whether there are some difficult attributes or behaviors that several people have in common. These may be characteristics you do not want to accept because you have them yourself and do not like them. If so, list them below and identify why you dislike them in yourself. Bear in mind that you may steer clear of these characteristics in others in order to avoid being reminded that you also exhibit them yourself. If this is so, put a check mark next to these attributes or behaviors.

. . . .

. . . .

. . . .

. . . .

. . . .

. . . .

. . . .

D. Finally, consider how you can increase your ability to empathize with those people whose attributes or behaviors bother you. Write how you will change your relationship with each person.

. . . .

. . . .

. . . .

. . . .

. . . .

. . . .

. . . .

To be more successful in empathizing with others, try changing your own "difficult" behaviors. If you can change yourself, you will become more skillful in leading others to change as well. By using empathy, each of us becomes our own greatest teacher. In the end, that is the best gift we can give to ourselves and each other.

Trust Through Consistency

Recent revelations of corruption, immorality, and betrayal in the financial sector have created an urgent public demand for leaders who are above suspicion and consistently adhere to moral, ethical, and value-based behavior. The rash of publicly revealed scandals of fraud, both governmental and corporate, is accompanied by millions of undiscovered, uncounted infractions—cheating, evading, covering up, half-truths, and petty moral erosions—committed by the "little people." The slogan for these seedy times seems to be "But everybody does it!" Numb to scandal and corruption in high places, many have lost trust in their leaders, and have let cynicism take its place.

Leaders with integrity have an ethical constancy that can be counted on, even when their plans are in a state of evolution. They make sure there is no gap between their values and their behaviors. They are there when it counts and ready to support others when it matters. Their bottom line is to have the integrity to honor their commitments and promises.

Here is what Harold Williams, former president of the J. Paul Getty Trust, said when he spoke to Warren about his experiences as chairman of the Securities and Exchange Commission long before the SEC's failure to discover and monitor the corrupt practices of member corporations:

> If there is anything I feel good about [at the SEC], it's the way I came through in terms of my own personal values and my personal self. If you believe in your course, you gotta stay with it in terms of course and timing. I think it's tough at times—when the press are all over you and you start hearing from Capitol Hill and you know that even some of your own staff are feeding the stories and the corporate community is up in arms, and there were several times when it was all going that way and it gets kind of heavy. . . . But if you believe you're right, and you've got your own integrity—and I think that's where it really ends up—I mean: "Do you believe in what you're doing?"—And if you believe it you stay with it. I couldn't change course and still respect myself.

As Williams pointed out, leaders rely on their integrity to stay the course. It is a challenge, however, for leaders to be true to their values without seeming rigid, self-righteous, and unresponsive to shifting realities. Leaders do walk a fine line in today's volatile climate and thus must over-communicate to endlessly express, explain, extend, and expand on what their values are and how important ethical practice is to the success of the enterprise.

Transparency and Trust Are Linked

In the end, ethical, value-based organizations are led as integrated organisms that are in harmony with themselves. Their communications are transparent, both within the boundaries of their organizations and between themselves and their external constituencies. Trust and transparency are linked because without transparency, we don't believe what leaders tell us and we suspect that they are hiding what it is that they don't want us to know. If their communications are not transparent, we mistrust the justifications they give us for secrecy, and when they tell us that a lack of secrecy would empower our enemies, we don't believe them. In most cases, lack of transparency is the *real* enemy.

The emergence of ubiquitous digital technology has made transparency and the exposure of secrets much easier to achieve, but also more relentless and in some cases as dangerous as secrecy. More and more of our personal data are being stored electronically, and powerful search engines allow this swelling archive to be mined in a matter of seconds by anyone with access to the Internet.

While new technology is literally emancipating millions of people and continues to offer endless possibilities, it also ramps up the ambient level of anxiety in daily life as we become increasingly reliant on our personal digital assistants: cell phones, text messengers, pagers, and other beeping, glowing devices. Paradoxically, greater transparency has brought bewilderment along with enlightenment, and confusion along with clarity. Each new revelation, much as we long for it, reminds us that the ground is not solid beneath our feet. Although we have more information than ever, we feel less in control. Our world seems simultaneously more anarchic and more Orwellian, both more and less free.

The trust we seek in those who lead can be found only when they have integrity and determinedly advocate and deliver transparency in every aspect of organizational life.

Organizational Leaders Define Shared Values

Values are essentially integrity-based choices and priorities. They are expressed by what we do, what we do *not* do, how we do it, what we accept, and what we are not willing to tolerate. Leaders openly and publicly express their values, act on them repeatedly, and uphold them when challenged. These values shape their responsibility, express their optimism and foster their self-esteem, and define who they are as leaders.

Values, ethics, and integrity are at the heart of every organization, defining its identity and mission, and when such qualities are made explicit, leaders at every level know why they are there, what they want to achieve, and how to evaluate their results. When leaders encourage personal values and ethics, everyone reaches a higher common ground. A good example of such a leader is the former president of California State University at Northridge, Dr. Blenda Wilson. In an address that inaugurated her seven years as president, she intro- duced the concept of shared values at her university by clarifying the value of *having* values:

> If we believe in ourselves, we will find and create a vital and participatory community in which every student, faculty, and staff member is valued and respected, in which we recognize that we share common values as educated and ethical human beings, and in which the bonds of community are stronger than the habits of cultural ignorance. This is our fervent goal.
>
> If we believe in ourselves, we will create the kind of learning environment and campus community that will prepare our graduates for a lifetime of learning, ethical conduct, global sensitivity, and service. Those institutions that will succeed in achieving a 21st-century version of academic excellence will be those institutions that believe—in their students, in their communi- ties, in themselves—and as a consequence of that belief, will take risks and design radically new approaches to embracing the imperative of change.

As Dr. Wilson promised, a leader's commitment to explicit values can generate respect, responsibility, and social cohesion in an organization. It remains for each of us to clarify our values and to express them in a powerful way to those we wish to lead so they embrace them as their own.

Your Ethical Ten Commandments—An Exercise

Moses, one of the most powerful leadership archetypes in Western culture, led his people out of slavery by espousing freedom and personal responsibility. Troubled by corruption in his community, he delivered the Ten Commandments, a code of ethics written with the aim of achieving a just and humane society.

As a leader in your own life, you have the opportunity to identify and honestly live by your own code of ethics and reaffirm values to guide your actions. Using the metaphor of the Ten Commandments, you can define the ethical standards that will guide your leadership behavior. This exercise gives you an opportunity to discover your values and fine-tune your ethical code for yourself as a leader.

We suggest that you initially work on your own and only later share your results with others. In this way you will find your own voice as you complete the charts below. Later, you can enjoy the insights and perspectives of others, and engage in a dialogue regarding shared beliefs and values.

On the first chart, indicate the Ten Commandments you propose for your organization and include your leadership values. On the second chart, indicate the core behaviors that exemplify each commandment. For example, if you have a commandment to "do no work that contributes to the loss of life of another human being," your core behavior might be to make sure the products manufactured by your company do not produce any toxic waste that might be stored or dumped at a site where human beings would be harmed. Alternatively, if you have a commandment to "never cheat the company out of money," you may commit to double-checking your expense reports and your requests for reimbursement to make sure they are accurate and honest.

My Ten Commandments for Ethics and Integrity on the Job Are:

1. . . . .
2. . . . .
3. . . . .
4. . . . .
5. . . . .
6. . . . .
7. . . . .
8. . . . .
9. . . . .
10. . . . .

My Core Behaviors That Exemplify Each Commandment Are:

1. . . . .
2. . . . .
3. . . . .
4. . . . .
5. . . . .
6. . . . .
7. . . . .
8. . . . .

9. . . . .

10. . . . .

After completing these charts and determining your ethics and the behaviors that support them, share them with co-workers and encourage them to identify similarities and differences in values and behaviors in your workplace. Next, review the questions below to discover areas for improvement.

Questions to Consider

A. Which of the Ten Commandments is most strongly held by everyone at work, and how have these values been expressed?

. . . .

. . . .

. . . .

. . . .

B. Which commandments were *most* difficult to identify or *least* used to guide everyone's behaviors?

. . . .

. . . .

. . . .

. . . .

C. What have you and/or your colleagues noticed about one another's values, and about the willingness of each of you to take a stand for what you believe is the right thing to do?

. . . .

. . . .

. . . .

. . . .

D. How has your organization supported you in shaping your values, or in living by them on a day-to-day basis? How has the organization's expectations and/or culture hindered you?

. . . .

. . . .

. . . .

. . . .

The leaders of one innovative corporation identified shared values through a process involving the entire company's personnel, at all levels. After they had articulated their values, they asked everyone to identify behaviors that contravened these values and were alien to their successful work environment. A sharp decline in negative behaviors throughout the organization resulted from this process. The company reached consensus on the following statement of its shared values:

> We, the executives, team leaders and team members of our company pledge, in our speech and actions, to uphold the following values, and invite others to remind us of them when we forget so they will become part of our everyday behavior:

1. To put the interests of our customers, creation of quality products, and organizational learning first, and work to make our company a true learning community.
2. To respect differences and diversity in race, gender, sexual orientation, culture, and opinion and personality.
3. To listen actively and respectfully to others, without yelling, blaming, intimidating or gossiping about disagreements.

4. To communicate directly, openly and honestly, and to tell the truth.
5. To take the initiative and encourage teamwork, inclusion, participation, consensus and risk taking.
6. To talk directly with people with whom we are having problems and respect them in doing so.
7. To focus on issues and interests rather than positions and personalities, and acknowledge work well done.
8. To take responsibility for our speech and actions, to follow the rules, and to be responsible for our behavior.
9. To model the behavior we expect from others and take pride in our work.
10. To hold these values as lasting and empowering guidelines for our ethical behaviors.

In the next step, everyone at the company identified behaviors that supported and were aligned with these values; that is, they identified behaviors they wanted to *encourage*, as well as behaviors that blocked or undermined these values and thus were behaviors they wanted to *discourage*:

ENCOURAGE	DISCOURAGE
Demonstrate the values	Labeling, stereotyping
Have a sense of humor	Making excuses
Exhibit empathy	Hierarchies
Respectful listening	Victimization
Take responsibility for our actions	Cliques and ganging up
Openness	Domination of others
Set goals and work toward them	Favoritism
Dependability	Interrupting
Kindness	Backbiting
Non-violence	Whining

Objective thinking	Controlling
Praising others	Cheating/stealing
Pride in your work	Favoritism/inequality
Employee-led meetings	Stereotyping
Recognize others' achievements	Exclusion
Consensus building	Arbitrary decision making
Positive criticism	Disparaging remarks
Same rules apply to everyone	Gossip
Relinquishing control	Retaliating
Active listening	Disrespect
Checking for understanding	Fear of expression
"I" messages	Negative labels
Ability to laugh at ourselves	Ask the source
More TGIFs (more playtime)	"It's gotta be my way"
Maintain sense of humor	Yelling and pointing fingers
Reflection, mediation	Racial slurs and sexual slurs
Equality	Physical and emotional abuse
Random acts of kindness	
Model desired behaviors	
Listen with heart	

As you expand your capacity to build trust through integrity, consider the shared values expressed by the leaders at every level of this company and the behaviors they wish to encourage. You may wish to adopt some of their ideas or to refine or further develop them for your own organization.

Leaders create "ethical capital" through a shared process that increases internal unity, morale, coherence, pride, and integrity among all employees. The real value of having values is that we consistently act with integrity—not because we are told to do so, or even because we are trying to do things right, but rather because it is who we *are* and how we choose to express ourselves as leaders. The true test of a leader's integrity is a code of ethics that guides everyday behaviors and builds trusting relationships with others.

Dr. Martin Luther King Jr., in a letter he wrote from a jail in Birmingham, Alabama, where he was incarcerated for upholding his value of civil rights for all people, eloquently described the price we pay if we do not live our values and do not take responsibility to do the right thing:

> I am coming to feel that the people of ill will have used time much more effectively than the people of good will. We will have to repent in this generation not merely for the vitriolic works and actions of the bad people, but for the appalling silence of the good people. We must come to see that human progress never rolls in on wheels of inevitability. It comes through the tireless efforts and persistent work of men willing to be coworkers with God, and without this hard work, time itself becomes an ally of the forces of social stagnation. We must use time creatively, and forever realize that the time is always ripe to do right.

For most leaders, Dr. King's call for tireless efforts to live by one's values permeates their entire lives. In Chapter 8 you will learn how to create a powerful link between your intentions and your actions. When you do so, you will increase the congruence between your values and the results that you produce in your life.

8 Realizing Intention Through Action: Competency Six

It is not power that corrupts but fear. Fear of losing power corrupts those who wield it and fear of the scourge of power corrupts those who are subject to it.

—**Aung San Suu Kyi**
Statement delivered when she was placed under house arrest
in Burma for the second time in 2003

AUNG SAN SUU KYI, THE BURMESE RECIPIENT OF THE NOBEL PEACE Prize in 1991, knew well of the dangers associated with the corruption of power, having been under house arrest from 1989 to the present day for taking courageous stands for democracy. As she withstood the dictatorial generals who imprisoned her and endangered her country, she became a worldwide symbol—not only of democracy and freedom but also of leadership and integrity.

When we search for leaders we can trust, we find talented people who have integrity, enormous talent, intelligence, and original minds. They see things differently, spotting the gaps in what we think we know. They have a knack for discovering interesting, important problems and they have the skills to solve them. They want to do the next thing, not the last one. They see connections. They have broad interests and multiple frames of reference. They are not so immersed in one discipline that they can't find solutions in others. They are committed to creating a future worth having, and they lead us to it.

These visionary problem-solvers can no more stop searching for improved relationships and better ways of doing things than they can stop breathing. They have the tenacity to accomplish valuable results and bring an authenticity and integrity to the process. As we look to these leaders to guide us, we ask them to address the challenges that are embedded in some troubling questions:

- How can we create space in our already clogged work-lives for the philosophy, metaphysics, and critical thinking that will enable us to rapidly enrich and renew ourselves?
- How can we design organizations that are committed to integrity, lifelong learning, growth, and continued revitalization?
- How can we provide learning experiences that increase integrity and stimulate the cognitive, emotional, and interpersonal competencies of sustainable leadership in the "new economy"?
- How can we give employees a passion for the moral and ethical consequences of their actions?

To address these questions and stimulate powerful responses to the challenges they represent, leaders must remain open to new experiences, vital information, and their own inner voices to take actions that are true to the ethical standards they hold dear.

Leaders Make Good Judgments

The judgment calls of leaders are not single-point-in-time events like those made by umpires and referees in the midst of their fast-moving games. Leaders do not quickly forget their decisions and move on to the next play; rather, after they make a judgment, they understand that its impact continues to the successful realization of their intentions through action.

When we observe truly effective leaders, we notice that they engage in three separate phases of judgment calls:

1. *Preparation.* During this phase, leaders identify and frame the issues and read the early signs that will require a judgment call. They name the issues, set clear parameters for the decision, and provide a context in which they align team members to understand why the call is important. They mobilize key stakeholders, inviting their input and harnessing their energies. Wise leaders habitually sense, frame, and articulate the issues so that they are prepared for a judgment call that may occur at any moment.

2. *Decision-Making Based on Storyline.* The chances of making an effective judgment call are vastly increased when leaders project a storyline that will inform and explain the action. A suitable storyline includes the organization's identity and mission and also expresses the leader's vision for the future. It articulates and reinforces shared values, and leads to the achievement of shared goals. Leaders evaluate possible consequences and alternate scenarios that will result from any decision. They measure it against their storyline so they and their followers know what action to take. In short, they proactively make excellent judgment calls.

3. *Implementation.* No judgment call is worth the effort if it does not produce the leader's intended results. Leaders mobilize and align the organization to action by framing the implementation correctly and compellingly. After leaders set a context for action, they stand by their decisions to bring them to fruition. If their judgments are off-base and they cannot mobilize their team, they rapidly realign with their values, reconsider the parameters of their decision, reformulate the problem, and redefine the goals to motivate others to produce the desired results.

As leaders implement these three phases, they focus on *people*, *strategy*, and *crisis response* when making decisions that will realize the greatest contribution to the survival and wellbeing of their organization:

1. *People.* When making decisions with and for others, leaders are better able to implement sensitive and wise judgment calls about the people involved if they set a sound direction and inspire the key players to join in their plans for the future.
2. *Strategy.* Leaders in any organization operate much like generals mapping advances or retreats for their troops. When they lead by strategies that resonate with their teams, their followers implement tactics that achieve success. When leaders realize that their strategies and tactics are not headed for success, they create new plans to achieve victory.
3. *Crisis Response.* When the stakes are high and a crisis looms, leaders not only confront the threat of a disaster but also face the possibility of public humiliation. The good news is that the disastrous consequences emanating from "bad calls" often become obvious so quickly that leaders can recoup, redirect, and redeem the situation and save their own reputation.

There is no denying that judgment calls are complex leadership behaviors that are influenced by personal style, and frequently depend on luck and on the vicissitudes of history. Indeed, judgment is at the core, the nucleus of leadership, and it matters greatly in determining what outcomes are produced and how they are achieved.

Improving Judgment Calls—An Exercise

Leaders who consider people, strategy, and crisis response increase their chances of making good judgments. Those who succeed in making the right decisions have certain characteristics that pertain to good judgment. As you review these characteristics, apply them to decisions that await you in your personal or professional life, or apply them to those that you may face in the future.

Characteristics to Consider

A. Leaders identify critical judgment calls and do not shy away from making them.

Good leaders discern when crucial decisions are needed, and they have the ability to sense what is critical to solving problems, framing the issues, and developing stories that will mobilize others to join them.

What is a significant judgment call you must make in your work, your family, your community, or your society?

. . . .

. . . .

. . . .

. . . .

. . . .

. . . .

. . . .

How will you involve others so that they will accept your decision and join you in realizing your intentions?

. . . .

. . . .

. . . .

. . . .

. . . .

. . . .

. . . .

B. The best leaders have a moral compass that guides their decisions.

Good leaders have a deep and abiding sense of right and wrong. They are clear about their stand on key issues long before they are forced to make a tough judgment call. Leaders with character consider the greater good before their own self-interest.

What are the moral guidelines and ethical values that inform your judgment calls, and how might you apply them to a decision you must make?

. . . .

. . . .

. . . .

. . . .

. . . .

. . . .

. . . .

C. The best judgment calls by leaders are informed by the best knowledge.

The leaders we trust make decisions based not only on intuition but also on the best knowledge available, and they apply it to finding the best solution possible. They accumulate a knowledge base and tap into it when their decisions influence the lives and livelihoods of others. They know that the success of their own careers and the sustainability of their organizations ride on their calls.

What blind spots will you illuminate with accumulated knowledge so that you will make informed and balanced decisions?

. . . .

. . . .

D. Leaders get the right people on their team and develop up-and-comers who can help them fine-tune their judgment calls.

Leaders who show good judgment aren't just having a series of lucky "aha" moments. Rather, they attract the right people, and seriously consider their feedback in evaluating past judgments as well as shaping future decisions.

Who are new leaders in your life whom you can help to develop, and who will assist you in expanding your knowledge base? How will you invite them to join you?

. . . .

. . . .

. . . .

. . . .

. . . .

. . . .

. . . .

Leaders with these characteristics consistently make their judgment calls within the context of a compelling ethical vision. As they powerfully communicate their vision, they effectively realize their intentions in concert with the actions of those around them.

Leaders Communicate Powerful Visions

Your vision can be a powerful force for change if you make it accessible and inspiring to others. If you intend to transform your vision into reality you must communicate it so that others get it.

It is not easy to bring a dream to reality. Good leaders perceive possible stumbling blocks and minefields that may stand in the way of their successes, yet they know that their deep and profound commitment to their vision, clear goals, winning strategies, and focused actions will realize their intended results. When passion drives them to make their dreams real, nothing can stand in their way.

W. H. Murray beautifully describes the force of commitment and passion in making a vision come true in his description of the Scottish Himalayan Expedition's success in climbing the highest peaks in the world:

> *Until one is committed there is hesitancy, the chance to draw back,*
> *   always ineffectiveness.*
> *Concerning all acts of initiative (and creation),*
> *   there is one elementary truth,*
> *   the ignorance of which kills countless ideas and splendid plans:*
> *That the moment one definitely commits oneself,*
> *   then Providence moves too.*
> *All sorts of things occur to help one*
> *   that would never otherwise have occurred.*
> *A whole stream of events issues from the decision,*
> *   raising in one's favor all manner of unforeseen incidents and meetings*
> *   and material assistance, which no man could have dreamt*
> *   would have come his way.*
> *I have learned a deep respect for one of Goethe's couplets:*
> *"Whatever you can do, or dream you can, begin it.*
> *Boldness has genius, power, and magic in it."*

In difficult times, when peaks seem impossible to reach, we require leaders who are clear about their commitments and openly and honestly affirm them, no matter the challenges they face. They infuse these commitments with a passion that makes them real.

Our colleague Dr. Noreen Clark, the former dean of the University of Michigan's School of Public Health, has had a passionate vision to which she has been committed for most of her long career as a leader in the field of public health. Specifically, she has a vision of healthcare systems that effectively and consistently serve the needs of poor families, especially those with chronic diseases such as diabetes, asthma, and cancer. Dr. Clark has realized this vision in the organization she created several years ago, which is devoted to research, policy development, and education for the management of chronic disease. She has powerfully, passionately, and consistently articulated her vision in speeches, articles, funding grants, and discussions with her colleagues:

> We aspire not only to broaden society's lens regarding the problem of chronic disease, but also to equip managers (individuals, families, systems and communities) with the skills necessary to enhance the well-being and quality of life of those who must live with a chronic condition and need quality healthcare services.

Noreen's passionate commitment to this vision and her skill in communicating it to attract grants from funders, colleagues' expertise, and partnerships with makers of policy have enabled her and her team to realize the joy of making a difference in the lives of the many families whom her organization has served by transforming their healthcare.

Passionate Commitments—An Exercise

If you are not conscious of your convictions, you cannot be strategic about achieving them or attracting others to join you. You may even alienate potential supporters if you are blind to your passions and cannot translate them into reality. This exercise offers an opportunity to discover your passionate commitments and to articulate them in such a way that you will gain the support of others. Before you identify these commitments, think about which of them you feel so passionately about that you would take a risk to uphold them. In the face of daunting opposition, consider which of your passionate commitments are part of your core identity.

Activities to Consider

A. Create a history of your life's passions and commitments. Include those you have long known and taken a stand to achieve as well as those you were unaware of before developing as a leader.

. . . .

. . . .

. . . .

. . . .

. . . .

. . . .

. . . .

B. Identify passionate commitments that you have expressed in words and deeds as well as those you hold privately and have kept to yourself.

. . . .

. . . .

. . . .

. . . .

. . . .

. . . .

. . . .

C. Describe the ways in which family, friends, and colleagues either support or limit you when you try to express your passions.

. . . .

. . . .

. . . .

. . . .

. . . .

. . . .

. . . .

D. Identify the passionate commitments you intend to express more openly and consistently in your life and in your work.

. . . .

. . . .

. . . .

. . . .

. . . .

. . . .

. . . .

As you review these commitments, ask your colleagues, relatives, and friends if they can guess your passions. Discuss their perceptions and learn more about how you are perceived by those who are close to you. If you are working with a team, share your observations with the members. Ask them to tell you about their own commitments. Notice the range of commitments expressed throughout the team. Discuss how team members can support one another so that each person can more openly express his or her passions. Discuss how you can successfully integrate and express your own commitments in your work environment and with your team.

Leaders Translate Commitments into Goals

A wise ancient proverb reminds us that if we do not know where we want to go, any road will take us there. Thus, it is best to be clear about our goals if we want to find the road to the results we intend to produce. Having a vision is an important beginning, but without clear goals that can be communicated, measured, and acknowledged when achieved, we are in danger of roaming in circles and never accomplishing anything at all.

It may be possible to achieve some of your goals in the short term; others will take longer, perhaps a lifetime. For example, if your vision is to be more respected and effective as a communicator, your short-term goal may be to discover the diverse perspectives of your colleagues on a specific problem that all of you face. A long-term goal may be to change your communication patterns so you consistently and clearly let others know about your expectations. If you identify your short-term goals and accomplish them, you can build longer-term goals and, ultimately, realize your vision.

Setting Goals to Realize Commitments Through Action— An Exercise

By taking the following steps, you will identify six goals to which you can commit during the next year. These goals will enable you to realize your intentions through your actions and bring you closer to reaching your vision.

A. Recall the personal vision you created in Chapter 5 and picture yourself as having realized everything you envisioned for yourself. Imagine where you will be located when you've achieved this vision as well as how you will feel, what you will be doing, who will be with you and what you will accomplish. Describe what you see on the next page.

My Vision for Myself

. . . .

. . . .

. . . .

. . . .

. . . .

. . . .

. . . .

B. List six key goals you will have achieved in one year toward realizing your vision for yourself.

The Six Goals I Will Achieve in One Year to Realize My Vision

Limit yourself to identifying six goals because if you have more you may be overwhelmed, and with less you may not get to where you want to go.

1. . . . .

2. . . . .

3. . . . .

4. . . . .

5. . . . .

6. . . . .

C. Your goals should be objectively measurable so that the results you produce are clear to you and others. Because it is important to know when you have achieved your goals, please specify the measurements by which you will evaluate your success.

Measures I Will Use to Evaluate My Success for Each Goal

1. . . . .

2. . . . .

3. . . . .

4. . . . .

5. . . . .

6. . . . .

D. Describe the fallback positions that you will use if you fail to achieve your goals. Once you see your fallback positions, you can decide how you will recover from any failure you might face by reformulating your goals and devising new strategies to achieve success.

My Major Fallback Positions

1. . . . .

2. . . . .

3. . . . .

4. . . . .

5. . . . .

6. . . . .

   Share your goals with colleagues and ask them to give you their feedback. You might ask them for their perceptions of the following: Do your goals support your vision? Are they achievable in one year? How will you measure your success? Are the goals worth accomplishing, and worth the effort? Do you notice any overlaps or similarities with the goals of others? If so, how can you support one another in successfully achieving them? These questions and their responses will take you to the challenging task of formulating strategies for success.

Leaders Think Strategically

Leaders know that "when you are the lead dog, the scenery always changes." Leaders who are out in front have, by definition, unique perspectives; they know where they and the team are headed and how they are going to get there. Out of necessity these "lead-dogs" think strategically and creatively to design solutions to problems that have not yet been manifested to others. Their strategies empower them to move out of reactive modes and enable them to take the initiative in dealing with complex problems. They can then organize others to engage in creative and strategic thinking.

Leaders develop strategies to achieve goals in the service of a compelling vision. To create their strategies they consider many variables, including shared values, human relationships, organizational cultures, costs of materials, timelines, and logistics. Successful strategists motivate others to join their effort and to implement their plans based on agreed-upon tactics.

The first step in planning a strategy is to be clear about the starting point of the effort. Leaders assess the strengths of their initial positions, the resources they have at hand, and the allies they can count on to join their efforts. They evaluate their choices—altering, connecting, compromising, revising, and imagining the end results they plan to achieve. They are perfectly clear about their beginning position as well as about where they want to end up.

As a part of their strategic thinking, leaders explore, elaborate, revise, and map alternate routes, taking into account contingencies, possible pitfalls, and dangerous traps. They are aware of the rewards awaiting them along the way, and of the satisfaction they will find when they reach their goals. They identify resources they will need to have available to support their efforts, and before they begin they systematically determine how they will secure these resources for the duration of the effort. They know who their allies are in advance of taking action, and they invite them to join their well-formulated strategy before it begins.

Finally, leaders create, revise, and review a map of their strategy with objective eyes; their aim is to locate soft spots, potential pitfalls, and dangerous turns in the plan so that they can eliminate possible failures and protect themselves from defeat. In addition, throughout the strategic process, leaders harness their passion and commitments to the achievement of their goals and inspire their colleagues to join their winning strategy.

Strategy Mapping—An Exercise

A *strategy map* is a powerful leadership tool for achieving your goals and realizing your organizational and personal visions. To create a strategy map that will guide your efforts and expand your leadership repertoire, respond to the questions below and discuss them with your colleagues. After that, you can make a plan of action.

These preliminary questions will reveal the information that will guide you in creating your strategy map.

Questions to Consider

A. What is one key goal you are committed to reaching in a year?

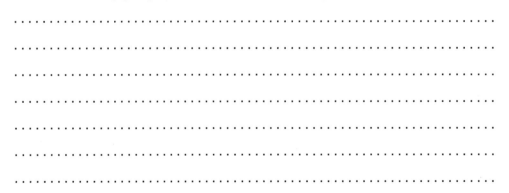

After you have stated your goal clearly, identify a starting point for the strategy that will take you to your goal. For example, if you have the goal of increasing the diversity of staff in your organization, especially that of staff in leadership positions, your starting point might be to make an assessment of the pool of eligible candidates who are being considered for new or existing leadership positions, or to conduct an evaluation of any advertisements, internal or external to the organization, for available positions.

In this example, you may discover that qualified candidates-of-color are reluctant to apply for a job in the organization because very few staff or leaders are people with whom they can identify. Perhaps you will discover that the personnel department is not enthusiastic about recruiting candidates-of-color. On further investigation, you might realize that you do not know how many positions will be open for hiring or promotion this year. Perhaps the organization's advertisements mentioning openings, interviews, and other aspects of the hiring process have hidden biases that put off those candidates you wish to recruit. Or perhaps you want to create a talent pool of candidates already in the organization from whom leaders may be selected in the future. Your strategic starting point will reveal how to proceed.

B. What is your strategic starting point for achieving your goal?

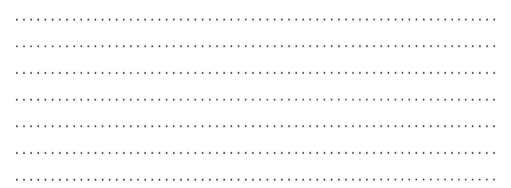

The next steps in creating a strategy map are to make a clear assessment of your allies and to recognize the available resources that are at your disposal. Continuing our example, you might want to find out who in the personnel department is receptive to achieving your goal of increasing diversity; perhaps you can invite this person to join you in enlarging the pool of qualified candidates-of-color, or in supporting candidates to apply for available positions. You might decide to seek help from someone in the finance department to determine the financial cost of your recommended recruitment process. You might seek support from the legal department to project figures that show possible reduced legal expenses for fewer claims of discrimination. You might look for assistance from public relations in launching a new recruitment effort. You might identify other organizations where similar goals have been achieved and recruit allies to prove that it can be done.

In other words, for the strategy to be successful, you must be in partnership with potential allies from many areas within and outside your organization.

C. Who are your potential allies, and what must you do or say to be successful in recruiting them join your team?

. . . .

. . . .

. . . .

. . . .

. . . .

. . . .

. . . .

Your strategy map should include the necessary resources to achieve the goals you have identified. Resources may come in many forms, including financial assistance, the approval of powerful people, access to decision-makers, and dedicated staff who will work with you to achieve your goals. You might also seek the approval of the CEO, or ask for support from the legal or accounting departments to estimate the costs to the organization if your goal is *not* achieved.

D. What resources are currently available to you in this project, and what additional resources do you need to be successful?

. . . .

. . . .

. . . .

. . . .

. . . .

. . . .

. . . .

After you have responded to these questions and discussed them with colleagues, you will be ready to create a strategy map to achieve your goals. Strategies are useful tools that will keep you on course and help you focus on a variety of effective tactics to deliver results.

Creating a Strategy Map to Achieve Leadership Goals

Using the model that follows, create a strategy map for achieving your goal. In the lower left-hand corner identify your starting point, and in the upper right-hand corner write your goal. Map A offers an example of a straightforward strategy that connects the starting point and the goal with a direct route that is the shortest possible distance between the two points. If a more circuitous route is required, your strategy will look more like Map B.

Your allies and resources should appear on your strategy map, as indicated on both Maps A and B. Place your allies above your strategy line and your resources below it. Notice that your strategy map can give you a clearer idea of how to achieve your goal and what support is needed. If you are working with others, ask everyone to join you in drawing a map together on large pieces of flipchart paper or on a whiteboard. If you are working on your own, you can use the strategy map worksheet we have provided. Share your strategy map with colleagues, and do a reality-check with them.

Strategy Map

GOAL:

ALLIES:

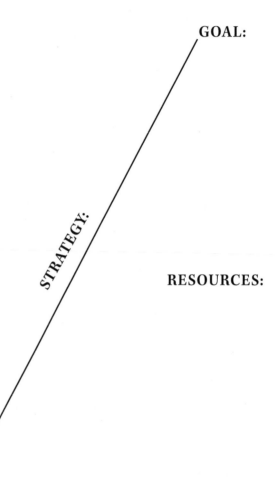

STRATEGY:

RESOURCES:

STARTING POINT:

Map A

GOAL:
Increased Positions Filled
with People-of-Color

ALLIES:

Other Organizations with Experience

Executives Who Support the Goal

Line Managers Who Want to
Hire People-of-Color

Individuals in Personnel Who
Support the Goal

STRATEGY: Have the Personnel Department Commit to the Goal and Work Toward Achieving It

RESOURCES:

Travel Money for Candidates

Funds for Special Recruitment

Recruiters and Head Hunters
with Good Contacts

Funds for Special Meetings
to Create Buy-in for Goal

STARTING POINT:
1 Percent of Staff and Executives
Are People-of-Color

GOAL:
Increased Positions of Staff
and Executives Filled
with People-of-Color

ALLIES:

Individuals in Personnel
Who Support the Goal

Other Organizations
with Experience

Line Mamagers and Executives
Who Support the Goal

Trainers Who Can Do
Related Workshops

Have Personnel Commit
to the Goal and Work
Toward Achieving It

Create Understanding
of Problem

RESOURCES:

Funds for Recruitment,
Advertising, etc.

Travel Money for Candidates

Funds for Speakers and
Educational Programs

Funds for Special Meetings
for Education

Build Concern
for Problem in
Organization

STARTING POINT:
1 Percent of Staff and Executives
Are People-of-Color

Questions to Consider

A. Do your colleagues agree that the allies and resources you have identified are the best and most appropriate to the goal?
B. Do they believe that you have created a powerful strategy that can achieve your goal?
C. Have your colleagues noticed any obstacles, pitfalls, and dangers that you need to consider in pursuing your strategy?
D. Are your colleagues willing to support you, and if so, how?
E. What might you do to support them?

Power Is Inherent to Leadership

No discussion of leadership, or of how leaders translate visions into reality, would be complete without a reference to power. We often associate power with physical force, but it is a more complex dynamic than this. Moreover, there are many forms of power. Below we discuss power as it is associated with *coercion, identification, expertise, group, access, persuasion, inspiration,* and *empowerment.*

Coercive power is usually accompanied by a tangible reward for compliance or a penalty for noncompliance and is often based on physical, mental, or emotional threats. Followers may lose their freedom and autonomy in such instances.

In cases of power based on identification with an idea or a particular personality, followers may surrender their own identities when they unquestioningly copy leaders and blindly carry out their bidding.

Another kind of power comes with expertise, whereby followers respect or seek to attain the level of knowledge of an expert whom they perceive as having superior knowledge, experience, or skill.

In addition, there is the power of the group, influencing the members of a group to conform to the norms prescribed by the culture. Followers who give in to the group may be controlled by "groupthink."

There is power based on access to people, goods, and decision-making authority, and only those with personal contacts benefit. Followers may surrender their integrity to gain access to people, financial gain, or goods that they covet.

There is also the power of persuasion, which is based on compelling arguments or convincing demonstrations. In such instances, followers tend to embrace any bill-of-goods they are sold.

How have you experienced or expressed your own power in various circumstances? When you understand the history of your particular type of power and how you engaged with it, you can significantly influence your choices of the forms of power you will use as a leader. In the exercise that follows, identify the types of power you have known in your past along with the limits and opportunities of each type. Self-reflection in this exercise will enable you to choose the forms of power that are most effective in your development as a leader and in the realization of your intended results in concert with others.

Uses of Power—An Exercise

The chart below indicates the various types of power that are available to you. Remember a time when you used each type or experienced it being used by someone else. Describe the incident briefly, and reflect on the limits of each type of power as well as on the opportunities it created.

Coercive Power:

INCIDENT	LIMITS	OPPORTUNITIES

. . . .

. . . .

Power by Identification:

INCIDENT   LIMITS   OPPORTUNITIES

. . . .

. . . .

. . . .

Power from Expertise:

INCIDENT   LIMITS   OPPORTUNITIES

. . . .

. . . .

. . . .

Power of the Group:

INCIDENT   LIMITS   OPPORTUNITIES

. . . .

. . . .

. . . .

Power by Access:

INCIDENT   LIMITS   OPPORTUNITIES

. . . .

. . . .

. . . .

Power from Persuasion:

INCIDENT	LIMITS	OPPORTUNITIES
. . . .
. . . .
. . . .

Power from Inspiration:

INCIDENT	LIMITS	OPPORTUNITIES
. . . .
. . . .
. . . .

Power Through Empowerment:

INCIDENT	LIMITS	OPPORTUNITIES
. . . .
. . . .
. . . .

When you have completed your chart, share your responses with your colleagues and ask these questions:

- Which forms of power are more limiting and which open new possibilities?
- What uses are made of the different forms of power in your organization?
- Which forms of power are encouraged in your organization, and which are discouraged?
- What would have to change in your organization for inspiration and empowerment to be the most frequent form of power used?

As you will notice from your introspection in this exercise and your experience with power, the power that is available through inspiration and empowerment is the most satisfying to leaders and most successful in including those they hope will join them in their efforts. As you prepare to make your vision a reality, consider being a leader who empowers others as the form of leadership you will employ. To focus your thoughts on this concept, write a scenario that describes how you will use empowerment to achieve your goals and realize your vision. As you do so, you may want to return to the strategy that you previously devised and revise it to incorporate an inclusive, inspiring, and empowering approach.

Write the details of how you will enact your strategy, who will be involved, how you will inspire and empower them to join you, what everyone will contribute, and what results you will achieve when your strategy succeeds.

My Scenario for Success

. . . .

. . . .

. . . .

. . . .

. . . .

. . . .

. . . .

. . . .

. . . .

. . . .

. . . .

. . . .

. . . .

. . . .

. . . .

. . . .

. . . .

. . . .

. . . .

. . . .

This scenario may be useful as a document for communicating your intentions to your colleagues. You can share it with them to let them know what you want to achieve and how they can provide assistance.

Leaders Assess Themselves—An Exercise

Leaders are willing to be lifelong learners, and they continually apply themselves to mastering the six essential competencies of leadership we have identified and you have experienced in this book:

1. Leaders understand the *context* of their history, their current environment, and their values and goals.
2. Leaders know themselves through reflection, self-observation, and continued learning.
3. Leaders are skilled in creating a vision for the future that attracts and includes others.
4. Leaders communicate with meaning to inspire others to make passionate commitments.
5. Leaders are committed to maintaining trust through empathy, constancy, and integrity.

6. Leaders are skilled in translating intentions into reality through committed action.

As you approach the assessment instrument below, take a moment to reflect on these competencies and the lessons you have learned about yourself as a leader. Evaluate your skills in each competency on a scale of 1 to 5:

> *1 =*   *I do not demonstrate this behavior.*
> *2–3 =*   *I may try this behavior, but I am not skilled in it.*
> *4 =*   *I'm pretty good with this behavior, but I have some room to grow.*
> *5 =*   *I am extremely successful in demonstrating this behavior.*

The examples in this assessment are focused on your job-related functions. If you are not currently working in an organization and are a student or retired or unemployed, extrapolate from the examples and apply them to your classes, home life, volunteer work, or community activities. Your task is to rate your leadership talents in your work or in other activities and settings.

The Competencies of Leadership

Please assess your ability to master the leadership competencies listed below. Think of yourself in the third person, as if you were observing yourself from a distance, and indicate a rating of 1 to 5 for each competency as well as for the specific behaviors you wish to change or aspects of your performance in which you would like to improve.

The results of this assessment offer you a beginning for the next phase of your leadership development process. Your honest and perceptive analysis comprise your agenda for your continued learning. You might also ask a colleague or supervisor to review your assessment and to fill out a copy of the chart, giving you feedback and recommendations for your growth.

1. Masters the Context

RATING	COMPETENCY	IMPROVEMENTS
	Is aware of the major issues in the larger environment and their impact on decisions.	
	Critically synthesizes information from internal and external sources when solving problems.	
	Considers possible outcomes and alternative actions when making decisions.	
	Takes calculated risks to change the organization or the environment.	

2. Knows Self

RATING	COMPETENCY	IMPROVEMENTS
	Focuses on self-learning and on developing a learning environment for all staff.	
	Cultivates relationships and alliances with teams and leaders to meet employee needs.	
	Builds networks of colleagues to create professional learning communities.	

RATING	COMPETENCY	IMPROVEMENTS
	Views errors and mistakes as learning opportunities for leadership development of self and others.	
	Participates regularly in development opportunities as a leader and as a learner.	

3. Creates a Vision for the Future

RATING	COMPETENCY	IMPROVEMENTS
	Is clear about a vision for the future and articulates it powerfully.	
	Pursues opportunities and develops strategies consistent with this vision.	
	Helps individuals define personal aspirations and roles consistent with this vision.	
	Revisits this vision to revise it with input from others and to align strategies with it.	
	Is able to let go of past practices and expectations to create a future based on this vision.	

4. Communicates with Meaning

RATING	COMPETENCY	IMPROVEMENTS
	Practices empathetic listening and honest dialogue with all staff and colleagues.	
	Is willing to confront conflicts and pursue lasting resolution and completion of all the issues.	
	Is clear about having a unique voice and is able to make it heard by others.	
	Seeks feedback, and changes behavior based on feedback from others and lessons learned.	
	Constructively uses disagreements and conflicts to develop innovative, collaborative solutions	

5. Maintains Trust Through Integrity

RATING	COMPETENCY	IMPROVEMENTS
	Has clear values and communicates them through behavior and commitments.	
	Provides others with opportunities to learn from mistakes and problems.	

RATING	COMPETENCY	IMPROVEMENTS
	Values diversity and supports diversity at all levels of the organization.	
	Demonstrates behavior that is consistent with values, ethics, and standards for integrity.	
	Provides opportunities for others to demonstrate their talents and stretch their skills	

6. Realizes Intentions Through Action

RATING	COMPETENCY	IMPROVEMENTS
	Gets viable results and adds value to efforts by transforming strategies into action.	
	Assumes personal responsibility for improving organizational achievement	
	Questions all roadblocks to success and eliminates them.	
	Evaluates results to improve work processes and leadership skills.	
	Gives credit to others for their contributions by noting specific achievements.	

Inspiration and Empowerment: Conclusion

The ability to inspire and empower other people is characteristic of leaders who make a significant difference in our lives. They often do so by creating organizations and learning environments that have the following qualities:

- *People feel significant.* Everyone in the enterprise feels that they make a contribution to its success. They know that their work matters and that it has meaning and significance.
- *Learning and competence are rewarded.* Leaders value learning. They communicate the importance of revealing mistakes, rewarding feedback, and giving everyone a chance to figure out what to do next and how to do it differently so that they succeed.
- *Everybody feels that they are part of a community.* Where true leadership, teamwork, and unity are created, everyone is recognized and heard, and the relationships among team members create an empowering community.
- *Work is exciting.* Being on the job and making a contribution are stimulating, challenging, fascinating, and fun, and the values of the organization are seen as challenges for personal growth that are attainable through committed action.
- *Quality is valued.* Quality is one of the supreme values held by all; it is appreciated intuitively and contributes to the beauty of everyone's work.
- *Dedication produces results.* Dedication is the attracting force energizing high-performance systems that produce results and leave everyone feeling justifiably proud.

In closing, we hope that this book has offered a fruitful beginning for you in learning to lead and expressing your values and integrity as you build collaborative, democratic, inspired, and empowered organizations, families, communities, and societies. We hope that as you lead you will love your work, your life, and yourself. More we cannot wish you. . . .

ACKNOWLEDGMENTS

If we were to acknowledge every leader who touched our lives, the ones who inspired us to write about leadership and the ones who challenged us to become all we can be, we would have a list of names that would match this book in size, and then some.

We could fill an additional volume with the names of many students and colleagues with whom we have pondered questions and discovered new ideas about leaders and their leadership. Some of these women and men *are* cited in this book but since we are not able to name all our heroes and teachers in the time or space we have, we hope they know who they are and accept our thanks for their inspiration and wisdom.

We want especially to thank our partners in life, Grace Gabe and Ken Cloke, for their love and light, and we thank Ken for his loving editorial advice, his elegant language, and much more. Our assistants Marie Dolittle, Mark Buriaza, and Solange Raro each deserve special acknowledgments for enabling us in so many ways. Our thanks also go to Carolyn Thibault for her excellent index, to Andrew Wilhelms for his thorough and insightful bibliography, and, especially, to our editor Lara Heimert and her team of Brandon Proia, Michelle Welsh-Horst, and Christine Arden for their support in bringing this book to publication.

A SELECTIVE BIBLIOGRAPHY
OF RESOURCES ON LEADERSHIP
BY ANDREW WILHELMS

Allen, John, *Rabble-Rouser for Peace: The Authorized Biography of Desmond Tutu*, Simon & Schuster, 2006.

> Drawing from considerable research and total access to the Tutu family and their papers, including the use of new archival material, John Allen tells the story of a barefoot schoolboy from a deprived black township who became an international symbol of the democratic spirit and religious faith.

Antonakis, John; Cianciolo, Anna T.; and Sternberg, Robert J., *The Nature of Leadership*, 1st ed., Sage Publications, 2004.

> The first concise and integrated volume that addresses current issues in leadership research, including emerging topics such as gender, culture, and ethics.

Arendt, Hannah, *Origins of Totalitarianism*, Peter Smith Publisher, 1983.

> A comprehensive history of totalitarianism, from the rise of anti-Semitism in Central and Western Europe in the 1800s through the institutions and operations of Nazi Germany and Stalinist Russia.

Athos, Anthony, and Pascale, Richard, *The Art of Japanese Management*, Warner Books, 1982.

> A comparison of Japan's Matsushita Electric Company and ITT, concluding that the fundamental differences between U.S. companies and their Japanese competitors lie in managerial style and cultivated skills rather than in organizational structures or systems.

Barnard, Chester Irving, *The Functions of the Executive*, Harvard University Press, 1971.

> The first book to provide a comprehensive theory of cooperative behavior in formal organizations, analyzing the psychological and social factors that both motivate and impede cooperation.

Bass, Bernard, *Bass and Stogdill's Handbook of Leadership*, Free Press, 1990.

A reference book providing brief but thorough summaries of leadership research and thought.

Bennis, Warren G., and Thomas, Robert J., *Leading for a Lifetime: How Defining Moments Shape Leaders of Today and Tomorrow*, Harvard Business School Press, 2007.

A comparison of today's young leaders with those of their grandparents' era, concluding that "crucibles"—utterly transforming challenges and tests—either break or embolden potential leaders.

Bennis, Warren, and Nanus, Burt, *Leaders: The Strategies for Taking Charge*, 2nd ed., Harper-Business, 1997.

Through extensive interviews with business and public-sector leaders, the authors identify two common attributes of leaders: (1) the ability to give vision to their organizations, and (2) the ability to translate those visions into reality.

Bennis, Warren, *On Becoming A Leader*, 3rd ed., Perseus, 2003.

The author elaborates six key principles supporting the thesis that the two essential components of leadership are creating a vision and translating that vision into reality.

Bennis, Warren, and Biederman, Patricia Ward, *Organizing Genius: The Secrets of Creative Collaboration*, Addison-Wesley, 1997.

Rather than focusing on individual leaders, the authors examine "Great Groups," synergistic collaborations that have left an enduring legacy, and argue that the Great Group and its great leader create each other.

Bennis, Warren; Spreitzer, Gretchen M.; and Cummings, Thomas G., eds., *The Future of Leadership: Today's Top Leadership Thinkers Speak to Tomorrow's Leaders*, Jossey-Bass, 2001.

A comprehensive collection of essays from today's foremost writers on leadership. Topics include the role of ethics in contemporary leadership, who is "responsible" for leadership, and why bad leaders are tolerated.

Bennis, Warren; Goleman, Daniel; and O'Toole, James, *Transparency: How Leaders Create a Culture of Candor*, John Wiley and Sons, Limited, 2008.

This book provides practical, actionable, and critical advice on how leaders can achieve healthy honesty and openness. In three separate essays the authors explore the lightning rod concept of "transparency," which has fast become a buzzword not only in business and corporate settings but in government and the social sector.

Bennis, Warren, *Why Leaders Can't Lead: The Unconscious Conspiracy Continues*, Jossey-Bass, 1989.

Bennis attributes leaders' inability to take charge and lead to an unconscious conspiracy in contemporary society and offers new insights and a more clearly developed conceptualization of the failures of present-day institutions.

Buckingham, Marcus, and Clifton, Donald O., *Now, Discover Your Strengths: How to Develop Your Talents and Those of the People You Manage*, Free Press, 2001.

The book identifies thirty-four positive "personality themes" and describes how to build a "strengths-based" organization by reinforcing and leveraging strengths already present in the organization's human capital.

Burns, James McGregor, *Leadership*, HarperCollins, 1985.

A study of the history, theory, and practice of leadership, distinguishing between transforming leadership, which shapes and elevates the motives and goals of followers, and transactional leadership, which mobilizes resources to realize goals held by both leaders and followers.

Carlin, John, *Playing the Enemy: Nelson Mandela and the Game That Made a Nation*, Penguin Group (USA) Incorporated, 2008.

Carlin details how then-president Nelson Mandela used a sporting event—the Sprinkboks rugby team in the 1995 World Cup—to mend South Africa. He draws on extensive interviews with Mandela, Desmond Tutu, and dozens of other South Africans caught up in Mandela's momentous campaign and the Springboks' unlikely triumph.

Caro, Robert A., *Master of the Senate: The Years of Lyndon Johnson*, 1st ed., Knopf, 2002.

This book studies not only the pragmatic, ruthless, ambitious Johnson, who wielded influence with both consummate skill and "raw, elemental brutality," but also the Senate itself, which Caro describes (pre-1957) as a "cruel joke" and an "impregnable stronghold" against social change.

Cloke, Kenneth, and Goldsmith, Joan, *Thank God It's Monday! 14 Values We Need to Humanize the Way We Work*, Irwin Professional Publishing, 1997.

A call for a more humane and fulfilling work environment. The authors focus on practical organizational change and offer exercises to help integrate the title's 14 values into the workplace.

Cloke, Kenneth, and Goldsmith, Joan, *The Art of Waking People Up: Cultivating Awareness and Authenticity at Work*, Jossey-Bass, 2003.

A description of new ways of utilizing feedback to foster individual and organizational change, based on the belief that organizations should develop systems, processes, techniques, and relationships that affirm the intelligence and humanity of their employees.

Cloke, Kenneth, and Goldsmith, Joan, *The End of Management and the Rise of Organizational Democracy*, John Wiley and Sons, 2002.

The authors present a new context and paradigm for organizational democracy and guidelines for creating ubiquitous, linking leadership and streamlined, open, collaborative processes.

Cloke, Kenneth, *Conflict Revolution: Mediating Evil, War, Injustice and Terrorism*, Janis Publications, 2008.

> Cloke provides strategies for addressing the origins of conflict and techniques for resolving issues in interpersonal relations. Relevant topics include emotions, crime, labor management relations, prejudice, the environment, politics, education, and economics. His focus is on how to transform social, economic, and political conflicts and the institutions that house them to help save the planet.

Cloke, Kenneth, *The Crossroads of Conflict: A Journey into the Heart of Dispute Resolution*, Janis Publications, 2006.

> Arguing that all conflicts are "crossroads" and catalysts for learning, evolution, growth, and wisdom, the author demonstrates how to locate the root sources of conflict and remove the barriers to reconciliation, collaboration, and community.

Cloke, Kenneth, *Mediating Dangerously: The Frontiers of Conflict Resolution*, Jossey-Bass/Riley, 2001.

> Cloke ventures beyond traditional steps, procedures, and techniques of conflict resolution to reveal the engine that drives the process of personal and organizational transformation. In exploring the edges, boundaries, and possibilities of mediation, he analyzes dangerous conflicts to uncover hidden choices and opportunities for transformation.

Conger, Jay A., and Benjamin, Beth, *Building Leaders: How Successful Companies Develop the Next Generation*, Jossey-Bass, 1999.

> This book studies the experience of a variety of organizations, identifies three dominant approaches to leadership education, and provides a framework for organizations to apply them to cultivate leaders on an ongoing basis.

Conger, Jay A.; Spreitzer, Gretchen M.; and Lawler, Edward E. III, eds., *The Leader's Change Handbook: An Essential Guide to Setting Direction and Taking Action*, Jossey-Bass, 1998.

> The USC Leadership Institute and the Center for Effective Organizations convened some of the nation's top business theorists to present cutting-edge thought on leadership and change management.

Conner, Daryl R., *Leading at the Edge of Chaos: How to Create the Nimble Organization*, Jossey-Bass, 1998.

> This book addresses the organizational and human elements required for an organization to be nimble and able to adapt instantly to today's changes, including rapid globalization, technological innovation, and increasing pressure from shareholders.

Covey, Stephen, *The 7 Habits of Highly Effective People*, Running Press, 2000.

> The author asserts that true success is a function of both personal and professional effectiveness and focuses on practical application of new habits to achieve individual change.

Csikszentmihalyi, Mihaly, *Flow: The Classic Work on How to Achieve Happiness*, Rider & Co, 2002.

> An intriguing look at the age-old problem of the pursuit of happiness and how, through conscious effort, we may more easily attain it.

Culbert, Samuel A., *Mind-Set Management: The Heart of Leadership*, Oxford University Press (USA), 1996.

> This book provides a model for thinking about other people—about their self-interested motives and about their biased views of work events. Culbert advises managers at all levels on how to use psychology instead of manipulation to give more productive advice.

Damasio, Antonio R., *Descartes' Error: Emotion, Reason, and the Human Brain*, Harper Perennial, 1995.

> Damasio draws on neurochemistry to refute the Cartesian idea of the human mind as separate from bodily processes and to support his claim that emotions play a central role in human decision-making.

Deal, Terrence E.; and Kennedy, Allan A., *Corporate Cultures*, 1st ed., Basic Books, 2000.

> This book argues that distinct types of cultures evolve within companies with a direct and measurable impact on strategy and performance. Organizations, by their very nature, are social enterprises, with tribal habits, well-defined cultural roles for individuals, and various strategies for determining inclusion, reinforcing identity, and adapting to change.

DePree, Max, *Leadership Is an Art*, Doubleday, 1989.

> The author explores how executives and managers can build better, more profitable organizations by creating covenantal relationships where people are enabled to meet corporate needs through meeting one another's needs.

Didion, Joan, *Slouching Towards Bethlehem*, Farrar, Straus and Giroux, 1961.

> A collection of essays that chronicles and analyzes America in the 1960s and helps the reader grasp the factors at play with themes such as "the center does not hold" and "things fall apart."

Eccles, Robert G., and Nohria, Nitin, with James D. Berkley, *Beyond the Hype: Rediscovering the Essence of Management*, Harvard Business School Press, 1992.

> This book discusses the role of the individual manager in mobilizing organizational action and effectiveness, focusing on action, identity, and rhetoric as the keys to connecting words and action.

Ellis, Joseph J., *Founding Brothers: The Revolutionary Generation*, Alfred A. Knopf, 2000.

> An argument that the highly personal interactions of key Revolutionary War figures formed the foundation of the new republic, including similarities and differences in beliefs and goals that persist in our political discourse today.

Follett, Mary Parker, et al., *Prophet of Management: A Celebration of Writings from the 1920s*, Harvard Business School Press, 1996 (out of print).

    A collection of lecture essays written or given between 1925 and 1933 on such topics as authority, leadership, the role of the individual in groups, and the place of business in society.

Freud, Sigmund, *Group Psychology and the Analysis of the Ego of Sigmund Freud*, W. W. Norton & Co., 1974.

    Freud viewed individual and group psychology as inextricably linked, if not identical. This work examines the emotional bonds that bind groups together.

Gardner, Howard, *Changing Minds: The Art and Science of Changing Our Own and Other People's Minds*, Harvard Business School Press, 2004.

    This book examines the factors involved in changing minds on significant issues in politics, science, business, and art. Gardner identifies seven key elements, including reason, research, and real-world events, that are part of the decision-making process.

Gardner, Howard, *Five Minds for the Future*, Harvard Business School Press, 2007.

    Gardner delineates the kinds of mental abilities that will be critical for success in the twenty-first-century landscape of accelerating change and information overload.

Gardner, Howard, with Emma Laskin, *Leading Minds: An Anatomy of Leadership*, Basic Books, 1995.

    This book outlines a cognitive framework for leadership asserting that effective leaders share four characteristics, based on a study of eleven twentieth-century leaders as diverse as Margaret Mead and Mahatma Gandhi.

Gardner, John W., *On Leadership*, Free Press, 1989.

    This book is a comprehensive analysis of leadership concepts, including such aspects as power, motivation, commitment, leaders and followers, shared values, and institution renewal. The author discusses and distinguishes between leadership, status, and power.

George, Bill, *Authentic Leadership: Rediscovering the Secrets to Creating Lasting Value*, Jossey-Bass, 2003.

    The author believes that true leaders must have a purpose and understand why they are leading and outlines five important leadership qualities: purpose, values, relationships, self-discipline, and heart.

George, Bill, and Sims, Peter, *True North*, John Wiley and Sons, 2007.

    In this book, former Medtronic CEO Bill George and co-author Peter Sims share the insights they garnered from interviews with 125 of today's top leaders. *True North* shows how anyone who follows his or her internal compass can become an authentic leader.

Gergen, David R., *Eyewitness to Power: The Essence of Leadership, Nixon to Clinton*, Simon & Schuster, 2000.

>Based on the author's experience in a series of political administrations, this book examines what it takes to be a great political leader and describes seven leadership qualities of a great president; also applicable to leaders in other contexts.

Gladwell, Malcolm, *Outliers: The Story of Success*, Hachette Book Group USA, 2008.

>Why do some people succeed, living remarkably productive and impactful lives, while so many more never reach their potential? Through a compelling examination of the lives and histories of well-known "outliers" ranging from Mozart to Bill Gates, Gladwell challenges the belief in the "self-made man" and builds a convincing case for how successful people rise on a tide of advantages, "some deserved, some not, some earned, some just plain lucky."

Gladwell, Malcolm, *The Tipping Point: How Little Things Can Make a Big Difference*, Little, Brown & Co., 2000.

>The author compares mass behavioral change to epidemics and identifies dynamics that cause events by generating critical mass, or "tipping points," attributable to minor alterations in the environment and the actions of a small number of people.

Goleman, Daniel, *Emotional Intelligence*, Bantam Books, 1997.

>The author argues that traditional IQ measurements are narrow predictors of success and that "emotional intelligence" is a better indicator of human success.

Goleman, Daniel; McKee, Annie; and Boyatzis, Richard E., *Primal Leadership: Realizing the Power of Emotional Intelligence*, Harvard Business School Press, 2002.

>This work posits that leaders' actions account for 70 percent of employees' perceptions of their organizations and argues for "resonant leadership," which is built on emotional intelligence and results in leadership styles based on collaboration and inspiration.

Goleman, Daniel, *Social Intelligence: The New Source of Human Relationships*, Bantam, 2006.

>A groundbreaking synthesis of the latest findings in biology and brain science, revealing that we are "wired to connect" and the surprisingly deep impact of our relationships on every aspect of our lives.

Goodwin, Doris Kearns, *Team of Rivals: The Political Genius of Abraham Lincoln*, Simon & Schuster, 2005.

>Through this moving historical account, Goodwin offers insights into Abraham Lincoln's leadership style and his deep understanding of human behavior and motivation. She illustrates Lincoln's political genius by examining his relationships with three men he selected for his cabinet, all of whom were better-born, better-educated rivals, and better-known opponents for the Republican nomination in 1860: William H. Seward, Salmon P. Chase, and Edward Bates.

Goodwin, Doris Kearns, *No Ordinary Time: Franklin and Eleanor Roosevelt*, Simon & Schuster, 1995.

> Using the tools of both history and biography, Goodwin relates the story of how Franklin Roosevelt led the United States to victory against seemingly insurmountable odds and, with Eleanor's help, forever changed the fabric of American society. This book provides a brilliant account of how the isolationist and divided United States of 1940 became, within only five years, the preeminent economic and military power in the world.

Grove, Andrew, *Only the Paranoid Survive: How to Exploit the Crisis Points That Challenge Every Company and Career*, Currency/Doubleday, 1996.

> This book presents an argument that correct management of the "strategic inflection point"—a moment of massive change that requires an organization to adapt or fail—propels companies and individuals to greater success.

Hackman, J. Richard, *Leading Teams: Setting the Stage for Great Performances*, Harvard Business School Press, 2002.

> The author argues that it is not a leader's management style that determines how well a team performs but, rather, how well a leader designs and supports a team so that members can manage themselves. Hackman identifies what leaders can do to structure, support, and guide teams in a way that sets the stage for great performances.

Handy, Charles B., *The Age of Unreason*, Harvard Business School Press, 1991.

> The author describes profound developments in education, technology, business, and employment and argues that new kinds of thinking and organizations are required in order to turn these changes to our advantage.

Handy, Charles B., *The Age of Paradox*, Harvard Business School Press, 1995.

> This book identifies unintended consequences of intended change and describes guiding principles for coping with the challenges and paradoxes of modern life.

Handy, Charles B., *The Elephant and the Flea*, Harvard Business School Press, 2002.

> A personal memoir acknowledging capitalism's possibilities and failures. The author describes the movement away from reliance on large companies to reliance on self, requiring creativity and agility.

Heenan, David A., and Bennis, Warren, *Co-Leaders: The Power of Great Partnerships*, John Wiley and Sons, 1999.

> A study of successful partnerships comprising a dominant individual and a "number-two" person. The book argues for the importance of good lieutenants willing to forgo the spotlight to support an organization's success.

Heider, John, *The Tao of Leadership: Lao Tzu's* Tao Te Ching *Adapted for a New Age*, Humanics/New Age, 1985.

> The author draws on principles in the *Tao Te Ching* to offer inspiration and advice on how to develop as a leader.

Heifetz, Ronald A., *Leadership Without Easy Answers*, Belknap Press of Harvard University Press, 1994.

Heifetz's model of leadership is a social contract whereby constituents confer power and resources in return for leadership and guidance.

Heil, Gary; Bennis, Warren; and Stephens, Deborah C., *Douglas McGregor, Revisited: Managing the Human Side of the Enterprise*, John Wiley and Sons, 2000.

The authors apply the work of McGregor, MIT professor and one of the first business thinkers to focus on human capital, to current business realities and needs. Topics include motivation, commitment, cooperation, and performance.

Hill, Linda A., *Becoming a Manager: How New Managers Master the Challenges of Leadership*, Harvard Business School Press, 2003.

Managers succeed by learning how to lead rather than doing the work themselves. The book follows nineteen new managers through their first year to reveal the complexities of transition to management.

Kanter, Rosabeth Moss, *The Change Masters: Innovation and Entrepreneurship in the American Corporation*, Simon & Schuster, 1985.

The author asserts the importance of incorporating entrepreneurial principles and practices in organizations as a way of creating flexibility engendering innovation to manage change effectively.

Kanter, Rosabeth Moss, *When Giants Learn to Dance: Mastering the Challenges of Strategy, Management, and Careers in the 1990s*, Simon & Schuster, 1989.

The author argues that truly innovative organizations led the way in the turbulent 1990s, with the "giant" corporations shedding bureaucratic cultures and joining the post-entrepreneurial "dance."

Keegan, John, *The Mask of Command*, Penguin, 1988.

This book analyzes the idiosyncrasies of four very different commanders—Alexander the Great, Wellington, Grant, and Hitler—in order to characterize the nature of command and how it has evolved over time.

Kellerman, Barbara, *Re-Inventing Leadership: Making the Connection Between Politics and Business*, State University of New York Press, 1999.

The author looks at the similarities between political and business leadership and argues that business and political leaders must work together to solve the most challenging social, economic, and political problems.

Khurana, Rakesh, *Searching for a Corporate Savior: The Irrational Quest for Charismatic CEOs*, Princeton University Press, 2002.

In recent years, corporations have pursued charismatic individuals for their reputation and personality rather than their experience and skills, thereby artificially narrowing the pool of potential candidates, raising compensation, and increasing the likelihood of failure.

Kidder, Tracy, *The Soul of a New Machine*, Back Bay, 2000.

    This book tells stories of thirty-five-year-old "veteran" engineers in the late 1970s hiring recent college graduates and encouraging them to work harder and faster on complex and difficult projects, exploiting the youngsters' ignorance of normal scheduling processes while engendering a new kind of work ethic.

Klein, Gary, *Sources of Power: How People Make Decisions*, MIT Press, 1999.

    Klein studies how people make choices when faced with time constraints, limited information, and changing goals.

Kotter, John P., *A Force for Change*, Free Press, 1990.

    Kotter uses questionnaires and detailed case studies for insights into how corporations work. He distinguishes between managers, who execute by monitoring results against the plans, and leaders, who execute by motivating and inspiring people to overcome bureaucratic hurdles.

Kotter, John P., *The Leadership Factor*, Free Press, 1988.

    Kotter discusses the need for leadership at all levels of management. He considers how business is changing and the impact of these changes on leadership, makes recommendations, and discusses how to implement the recommendations.

Kotter, John P., *Leading Change*, Harvard Business School Press, 1996.

    The author argues that, for change to succeed, behaviors need to be altered. He describes common mistakes that prevent success and suggests eight steps for avoiding them.

Kotter, John P., and Cohen, Dan P., *The Heart of Change: Real-Life Stories of How People Change Their Organizations*, Harvard Business School Press, 2002.

    In this follow-up to *Leading Change*, the authors argue that companies often focus on changing how employees think about change rather than on how they feel. They introduce the "see-feel-change" process that inspires people to change their emotions by showing them powerful reasons for change.

Kouzes, James M., and Posner, Barry Z., *Credibility: How Leaders Gain and Lose It, Why People Demand It*, Jossey-Bass, 2002.

    The authors argue that leadership is based on relationship, and that relationship is dependent upon credibility. They offer six key disciplines and practices to strengthen a leader's ability to create and sustain credibility.

Kouzes, James M., and Posner, Barry Z., *Encouraging the Heart: A Leader's Guide to Rewarding and Recognizing Others*, Jossey-Bass, 2002.

    The authors believe that employees perform best when they are encouraged and their efforts are appreciated. They argue that "compassionate supervision" is becoming a critical part of management today and that the appreciation must be real, demonstrated with rewards, and tied to standards of excellence.

Kouzes, James M., and Posner, Barry Z., *The Leadership Challenge: How to Get Extraordinary Things Done in Organizations*, Jossey-Bass, 2002.

 The authors draw from interviews with 500 managers to build and illustrate a model of leadership, covering such topics as identifying and developing leadership qualities and turning commitment into action.

Krugman, Paul R., *The Conscience of a Liberal*, W. W. Norton & Company, 2007.

 Nobel Laureate Krugman discusses complex economic questions in the context of political choices by leaders. He makes the case for citizen involvement in government decisions to deal with the extreme inequality in contemporary United States.

Lawler, Edward E., and Worley, Christopher G., *Built to Change: How to Achieve Sustained Organizational Effectiveness*, John Wiley and Sons, 2006.

 Lawler and Worley provide a framework for how organizations can be "built to change" so they can last and succeed in today's global economy. They make the case for why organizations need to be better able to stimulate and facilitate change, and they identify practices and designs that organizations can adopt to reach this goal.

Leavitt, Harold J., *Corporate Pathfinders: Building Vision and Values into Organizations*, Dow Jones–Irwin, 1986.

 This model of the management process involves three steps: pathfinding (asking the right questions), problem-solving (analysis), and implementing (action).

Lencioni, Patrick M., *The Five Dysfunctions of a Team: A Leadership Fable*, John Wiley and Sons, 2002.

 A compelling fable with a powerful yet deceptively simple message that reveals five dysfunctions that go to the very heart of why teams, even the best ones, often struggle.

Lipman-Blumen, Jean, *The Allure of Toxic Leaders*, Oxford University Press, 2006.

 The author provides an analysis of what makes toxic leaders and why they are followed in times of crisis. The book presents a powerful warning against dangerous threats to democracy in our times.

Lipman-Blumen, Jean, *The Connective Edge: Leading in an Interdependent World*, 1st ed., Jossey-Bass, 1996.

 Lipman-Blumen examines the origin and evolution of the human need for leadership, details what is described as the Connective Leadership Model, and explores the empirical organizational results and philosophical implications of this new model. The book presents a complex design for a new leadership ideal—one that forms short-term coalitions to solve immediate problems and moves rapidly and adjusts easily to changing circumstances while taking a long-term perspective.

Lukacs, John, *Five Days in London: May 1940*, Yale University Press, 1999.

 A historical account of the period immediately preceding Winston Churchill's decision that Britain would fight Germany, chronicling Churchill's perseverance in the face of wide opposition.

225

Machiavelli, Niccolo, *The Prince*, 2nd ed., trans. Harvey C. Mansfield, University of Chicago Press, 1998.

    This book is considered by many to be the definitive translation of this classic guide to manipulative leadership.

Manchester, William, *A World Lit Only by Fire: The Medieval Mind and the Renaissance*, Papermac, 1994.

    An informal history of the European Middle Ages, structured into three sections: *The Medieval Mind*, *The Shattering*, and *One Man Alone*. In the book, Manchester argues that the Middle Ages were ten centuries of technological stagnation, short-sightedness, bloodshed, feudalism, and an oppressive church wedged between the golden ages of the Roman Empire and the Renaissance.

Mandela, Nelson, *Long Walk to Freedom: The Autobiography of Nelson Mandela*, Back Bay Books, 1995.

    In this autobiographical work, Mandela describes his early life, coming of age, education, and twenty-seven years in prison. The last chapters of the book describe his political ascension and his belief that the struggle continues against apartheid in South Africa.

Maslow, Abraham H., *Maslow on Management*, John Wiley and Sons, 1998.

    A highly influential writer on psychology and counseling, Maslow was widely known for his "hierarchy of needs." This book is the result of a journal written in 1962, when Maslow was hired to help give workers a voice in organizing production.

Mayo, Anthony J., and Nohria, Nitin, *In Their Time: The Greatest Business Leaders of the Twentieth Century*, Harvard Business Press, 2005.

    Based on a comprehensive Harvard Business School Leadership Initiative study, Anthony J. Mayo and Nitin Nohria present a fascinating collection of stories of the twentieth century's greatest leaders, from unsung heroes to legends like Sam Walton and Bill Gates. The book identifies three distinct paths these individuals followed to greatness: entrepreneurial innovation, savvy management, and transformational leadership. Through engaging stories of leaders in each category, the authors show how, by "reading" the context they operated in and embracing the opportunities their times presented, these individuals created, grew, or revitalized outstanding American enterprises.

McCall, Morgan W., and Hollenbeck, George P., *Developing Global Executives: The Lessons of International Experience*, Harvard Business School Press, 2002.

    The authors posit that the success of global businesses depends upon the quality of international executives developed through global experience. They highlight the key requirements and challenges of global leadership and emphasize the importance of experienced mentors.

McCall, Morgan W.; Morrison, Ann M.; and Lombardo, Michael M., *Lessons of Experience: How Successful Executives Develop on the Job*, Simon & Schuster, 1998.

    The authors interviewed senior executives in order to learn what experiences had the greatest impacts on their careers and what lessons were learned. They identify elements that maximize skill development and provide tools for evaluating the learning value of job assignments, as well as for creating jobs with higher development potential.

McCauley, Cynthia D.; Moxley, Russ S.; and Van Velsor, Ellen, eds., *The Center for Creative Leadership Handbook of Leadership Development*, Jossey-Bass, 1998.

    A comprehensive manual for individuals and organizations, describing the key elements of leadership development, focusing on six approaches to leadership development, and providing tools to help organizations evaluate their efforts.

McGregor, Douglas, *The Human Side of Enterprise: Annotated Edition*, Contributor Joel Cutcher-Gershenfeld, McGraw-Hill Professional, 2006.

    The timeless wisdom of Douglas McGregor describes a management style that nurtures leadership capability, creates effective teams, ensures internal alignment, achieves high performance, and cultivates an authentic, value-driven workplace. In this special annotated edition of the worldwide management classic, Joel Cutcher-Gershenfeld shows us how today's leaders have successfully incorporated McGregor's methods into modern management styles and practices.

Miller, Arthur, *On Politics and the Art of Acting*, Viking Press, 2001.

    One of the country's most prominent playwrights argues that the modern media have raised the level of acting ability required for political office. This book compares modern politicians from FDR to Clinton.

Moyers, Bill D., *Moyers on Democracy*, Random House, Inc., 2008.

    This collection of speeches offers a passionate examination of the principles and ideals that rightly provoke pride in America and the shortcomings that evoke shame. Moyers offers moving tributes to exemplars who upheld the highest ideals of democracy and simple human decency, including William Sloane Coffin, Hubert H. Humphrey, Lady Bird Johnson, and Barbara Jordan.

Nanus, Burt, *The Leader's Edge*, Contemporary Books, 1989.

    The author argues that leadership has been too preoccupied with the present at the expense of the future and with the internal environment at the expense of the external one. He describes seven interrelated "mega-skills" required to correct these faults.

Nohria, Nitin, *Driven: How Human Nature Shapes Our Choices*, Jossey-Bass, 2002.

    The authors present a sociobiological theory of motivation, claiming that humans possess four basic drives: to acquire, to bond, to learn, and to defend. Successful organizations give their employees opportunities to fulfill all of these drives.

O'Toole, James, *Executive's Compass: Business and the Good Society*, Oxford University Press, February 1995.

    This book provides business leaders with a practical compass to help them navigate the turbulent waters of social change and political conflict. It explores the philosophical and historical underpinnings of contemporary business problems, tracing their origins to the ideas of such great thinkers as Aristotle, Adam Smith, J. S. Mill, and Jefferson.

O'Toole, James, *Leadership A to Z: A Guide for the Appropriately Ambitious*, Jossey-Bass, 1999.

    O'Toole has compiled an anthology of real-life stories with topics including communication, effectiveness, and listening.

O'Toole, James, *Leading Change: Overcoming the Ideology of Comfort and the Tyranny of Custom*, Jossey-Bass, 1995.

    The author posits that only value-based leadership is powerful enough to break through the inertia of comfort and custom to overcome the pull of the modern world's many distractions.

O'Toole, James, and Lawler, Edward E., *The New American Workplace*, Macmillan, 2007.

    Following their groundbreaking 1972 study, *Work in America*, O'Toole and Lawler take a fresh look at how life at the office has changed in the last thirty-five years. Their not-so-startling conclusion is that the United States is attempting to implement tomorrow's competitive strategies with yesterday's managerial ideas and public policy infrastructure.

Palmer, Parker J., *The Courage to Teach: Exploring the Inner Landscape of a Teacher's Life*, Jossey-Bass, 1997.

    The author argues that good teaching is founded on the teacher's strong identity and integrity. Good teachers connect their students, their material, and themselves, enabling students to develop their own understanding of the world.

Parks, Sharon Daloz, *Leadership Can Be Taught: A Bold Approach for a Complex World*, Harvard Business Press, 2005.

    Parks shows how we can learn, practice, and teach the art of leadership in more skilled, effective, and inspired forms.

Pascale, Richard T., *Managing on the Edge: How the Smartest Companies Use Conflict to Stay Ahead*, Simon & Schuster, 1990.

    Pascale argues that modern management must embrace disequilibrium and transcend the old focus on control, stability, and avoidance of ambiguity.

Peters, Thomas, and Waterman, Robert, *In Search of Excellence: Lessons from America's Best-Run Companies*, Warner Books, 1988.

    In this classic book on management, the authors identify and examine successful American companies and synthesize eight principles for success.

Pfeffer, Jeffrey, and Sutton, Robert I., *The Knowing-Doing Gap: How Smart Companies Turn Knowledge into Action*, Harvard Business School Press, 1999.

    The authors argue that there is a gap between what many companies know they should do and what they actually do. They identify why companies fail to apply hard-earned knowledge and experience and suggest ways to create action.

Rhode, Deborah L., *Moral Leadership*, with contributor Warren G. Bennis, John Wiley and Sons, 2006.

    This is a comprehensive collection of essays from leading scholars in law, leadership, psychology, political science, and ethics to provide practical, theoretical, and policy guidance. The authors explore key questions about moral leadership: How do leaders form, sustain, and transmit moral commitments? Under what conditions are those processes most effective? What is the impact of ethics officers, codes, training programs, and similar initiatives? How do standards and practices vary across context and culture? What can we do at the individual, organizational, and societal levels to foster moral leadership?

Ridley, Matt, *Nature via Nurture: Genes, Experience, and What Makes Us Human*, Harper-Collins, 2003.

    Ridley asserts that the nature vs. nurture question itself is a "false dichotomy." Using copious examples from human and animal behavior, Ridley presents the notion that our environment affects the way our genes express themselves.

Riggio, Ronald E.; Chaleff, Ira; and Lipman-Blumen, Jean, eds., *The Art of Followership: How Great Followers Create Great Leaders and Organizations*, Jossey-Bass, 2008.

    This book examines the multiple roles followers play and their often complex relationship to leaders. With contributions from leading scholars and practitioners f rom the burgeoning field of leadership/followership studies, this groundbreaking book outlines how followers contribute to effective leadership and to organizations overall.

Rohatyn, Felix, *Bold Endeavors: How Our Government Built America, and Why It Must Rebuild Now*, Simon & Schuster, 2009.

    Rohatyn makes the case for rebuilding the infrastructure that goes with the major nuclear program the United States has supported for the last twenty-five years, from creating an energy grid to dealing with nuclear-waste disposal.

Rosen, Robert, with Brown, Paul B., *Leading People: Transforming Business from the Inside Out*, Viking, 1995.

    This book describes eight principles of leadership, illustrated with profiles of thirty-six of America's current notable leaders, and argues that the best, most effective leaders pay at least as much attention to principles and people as they do to profits.

Sample, Steven B., *The Contrarian's Guide to Leadership*, Jossey-Bass, 2002.

   A university president, the author offers insights and suggestions on leadership that often run counter to conventional wisdom.

Schein, Edgar H., *Organizational Culture and Leadership*, 2nd ed., Jossey-Bass, 1992.

   An organization's culture lies in shared assumptions, and a leader must decipher these assumptions. Ultimately, the leader must foster a "learning organization," which contains the cultural mechanisms to manage and diagnose itself.

Schein, Edgar H., *The Corporate Culture Survival Guide*, Jossey-Bass, 1999.

   The author describes corporate culture as the "learned, shared, tacit assumptions on which people base their daily behavior" and argues that the failure to address these assumptions is an important reason that many corporate acquisitions fail.

Senge, Peter M., *The Fifth Discipline: The Art and Practice of the Learning Organization*, Doubleday/Currency, 1990.

   The author proposes the "systems thinking" method to help a corporation to become a "learning organization," one that integrates at all personnel levels in differently related company functions to improve productivity.

Shakespeare, William, "Julius Caesar," *The Complete Works of William Shakespeare*, The Cambridge Edition Text, as edited by William Aldis Wright, Doubleday, Doran & Company, Inc., 1936.

   This play explores the anxieties caused by an uncertain succession of leadership. The central psychological drama is the struggle of the protagonist, Marcus Brutus, between the conflicting demands of honor, patriotism, and friendship.

Snook, Scott A., *Friendly Fire: The Accidental Shootdown of U.S. Black Hawks over Northern Iraq*, Princeton University Press, 2000.

   The author approaches the event from individual, group, organizational, and cross-level perspectives and employs a rigorous analysis based on behavioral science theory to account for critical links in the causal chain of events.

Sonnenfeld, Jeffrey, *The Hero's Farewell: What Happens When CEOs Retire*, Oxford University Press, 1998.

   How a company deals with a CEO's replacement usually has a profound impact on the company's future. The author identifies four major types of departure styles and outlines suggestions for smooth leadership transitions.

Spears, Larry C., and Lawrence, Michele, eds., *Focus on Leadership: Servant-Leadership for the Twenty-First Century*, Jossey-Bass, 2001.

   This book is a collection of essays on servant-leadership by prominent thinkers on leadership and management.

Stiglitz, Joseph E., and Bilmes, Linda, *The Three Trillion Dollar War: The True Cost of the Iraq Conflict*, Boydell & Brewer, 2008.

Nobel Prize winner Joseph E. Stiglitz and Harvard professor Linda J. Bilmes investigate the astronomical expenses that have been hidden from the U.S. taxpayer, the cost in lives and economic damage within Iraq, and the opportunity costs of what the U.S. taxpayer's money would have produced if it had been invested in the further growth of the U.S. economy.

Tapscott, Don, and Williams, Anthony D., *Wikinomics: How Mass Collaboration Changes Everything*, Portfolio Hardcover, 2006.

The authors explain the quickly changing world of Internet togetherness, also known as mass or global collaboration, and what those changes mean for business and technology.

Tichy, Noel, and Cardwell, Nancy, *The Cycle of Leadership: How Great Leaders Teach Their Companies to Win*, HarperBusiness, 2002.

Teaching and learning are the crux of effective leadership, and strong leaders foster both dynamics at all levels of the organization. This book provides specific information and strategies to guide organizations to build and maintain themselves as "teaching organizations."

Tichy, Noel M., and Bennis, Warren G., *Judgment: How Winning Leaders Make Great Calls*, Portfolio, 2007.

This book offers a powerful framework for making tough calls when the stakes are high and the right path is far from obvious. Tichy and Bennis show how to recognize the critical moment before a judgment call, when swift and decisive action is essential, and also how to execute a decision after the call.

Tichy, Noel, *The Leadership Engine: How Winning Companies Build Leaders at Every Level*, HarperBusiness, 1997.

Companies succeed when they have "good leaders who nurture the development of other leaders at all levels of the organization." The "leadership engine" created by this attention creates good leaders throughout the organization, all driving the organization in the same direction.

Tuchman, Barbara, *The Guns of August*, Ballantine Books, 1994.

Tuchman details the military decisions and actions that occurred leading up to and during the first month of World War I.

Tuchman, Barbara, *The March of Folly: From Troy to Vietnam*, MacMillan Library Reference, 1984.

A Pulitzer Prize–winning author examines folly in governments throughout history. She defines "folly" in this context as a government's pursuit of policies contrary to its own interests, despite the presence of viable alternatives.

Useem, Michael, *The Leadership Moment: Nine True Stories of Triumph and Disaster and Their Lessons for Us All*, Crown Publishing Group, 1999.

Nine dramatic stories about leaders in various fields and their responses to critical challenges.

Wills, Garry, *Certain Trumpets: The Nature of Leadership*, Simon & Schuster, 1995.

> Wills examines leadership as a mutually determined exchange between leader and follower. This concept is illustrated with sixteen biographies illustrating leadership in particular contexts.

Wren, J. Thomas, *The Leader's Companion: Insights on Leadership Through the Ages*, Free Press, 1995.

> A comprehensive collection of writings on leadership by a wide variety of experts and philosophers, from classic selections by Aristotle, Machiavelli, and Tolstoy to essays by modern experts such as James MacGregor Burns and Bernard Bass.

Yukl, Gary A., *Leadership in Organizations*, Prentice-Hall, 1981.

> A clear summary of basic issues for the new student of leadership. Topics include power and leader effectiveness, role, expectancy and adaptive-reactive theories, and determinants of effective group decisions.

Zaffron, Steve, and Logan, Dave, *The Three Laws of Performance: Rewriting the Future of Your Organization and Your Life*, John Wiley and Sons, 2009.

> This book outlines a proven system for rallying all of an organization's employees around a new vision and, more important, making it stick. The focus is on making such transformations permanent and repeatable, providing practical examples including Apple, Lockheed Martin, Reebok, BHP-Billiton, Johnson & Johnson, and Morgan Stanley.

INDEX